D0586096

Not Without You

Cricket in Conflict

Cricket in Conflict

Peter Wynne-Thomas
Peter Arnold

NEWNES BOOKS

Published by Newnes Books
84–88, The Centre, Feltham, Middlesex, England
and distributed for them by
The Hamlyn Publishing Group Limited
Rushden, Northants, England

First published 1984

ISBN 0 600 35706 6

Phototypeset by Input Typesetting Ltd, London
Printed in Great Britain at The Pitman Press, Bath

Contents

Bibliography and Acknowledgments

Several newspapers, journals and magazines have been quoted in the text, and the authors thank them and their contributors. The specialist journals, *Cricket, Cricket Quarterly, The Cricketer* and *Wisden Cricket Monthly* have proved especially valuable.

A number of books have also been quoted, and many others have proved of value in research. In many cases they provide a fuller account of a cricket conflict than is to be found in the relevant chapter or part of a chapter in this book, and they are recommended to those readers who wish to discover more on a particular topic. The present authors thank the authors and publishers of the following:

Bowen, R. *Cricket, A History of its Growth and Development throughout the World* (Eyre and Spottiswoode, London, 1970).

Caffyn, W. *Seventy-one Not Out* (Blackwood, London, 1899).

Carr, A. W. *Cricket with the Lid Off* (Hutchinson, London, 1955).

Close, D. B. *I Don't Bruise Easily* (Macdonald and Jane's, London, 1978).

Harris, Lord and Ashley-Cooper, F. S. *Kent Cricket Matches 1719–1880* (Gibbs, Canterbury, 1929).

Hawke, Lord *Recollections and Reminiscences* (Williams and Norgate, London, 1924).

Kilburn, J. M. *A History of Yorkshire Cricket* (Stanley Paul, London, 1970).

Larwood, Harold *Bodyline?* (Elkin, Mathews and Marrot, London, 1933).

Larwood, Harold *The Larwood Story* (W. H. Allen, London, 1965).

Le Quesne, Lawrence *The Bodyline Controversy* (Secker and Warburg, London, 1983).

Moyes, A. G. *Australian Cricket, A History* (Angus and Robertson, Sydney, 1959).

Nyren, John *The Young Cricketers' Tutor* (Effingham and Wilson, London, 1833).

Oldfield, W. A. *The Rattle of the Stumps* (George Newnes, London, 1954).

Stevenson, Mike *Illingworth* (Ward Lock, London, 1978).

Streeton, Richard *P. G. H. Fender, A Biography* (Faber and Faber, London, 1981).

Wardle, J. H. *Happy Go Johnny* (Robert Hale, London, 1957).

Wynne-Thomas, Peter *England on Tour* (Hamlyn, London, 1982).

The authors have also consulted various editions of: *Lillywhite's Cricketers' Companion, Lillywhite's Cricketers' Annual* and A. Haygarth's *Scores and Biographies*, as well as the still-flourishing *Wisden Cricketers' Almanack*.

The lines quoted on page 156 (with 'he' substituted for 'I') are from the poem 'Should Lanterns Shine' by Dylan Thomas, reprinted by permission of David Higham Associates, London.

Picture Acknowledgments

The photographs between pages 96 and 97 were supplied by Patrick Eagar (D'Oliveira, Illingworth and Boycott, Packer and Greig) and Keystone Press Agency Limited (Larwood bowling to Woodfull, McCarthy, Meckiff, Griffin, Jackman, Rowe). The remainder are from the archives of Nottinghamshire County Cricket Club.

Introduction

Rose-coloured spectacles have always been an essential part of any cricket follower's equipment. Now, when conflict is in almost every headline, the apparent tranquility of the past is in greater demand than ever and the nostalgia industry is reaping its own reward.

If the stage is ever reached when cricket does not reflect the times in which we live, then the game will be dead. It will be like one of those carefully preserved villages, which are so beloved by certain sections of the public, artificial and lifeless.

The purpose behind this book is to demonstrate that cricket has always been beset by conflict and has not only survived but more often than not been improved by the experience. Where would the game be now if the traditionalists had won the day and over-arm bowling was still banned, if the paternalism and the wages structure of the so-called 'Golden Age' was still strictly enforced, if the players did not continue to use all their ingenuity to beat their opponents, even if it means testing the letter of the Laws and in some cases forcing alterations?

An unfortunate consequence of the fact that cricket is very much alive is the use to which politicians are trying to put the game in the context of South Africa. The participation of that country's representatives in an international 'Club-ball' championship, say, would hardly make the television news, but unlike Club-ball, cricket has not become fossilised, so the fans have to suffer the inconvenience of living in the twentieth century. This kind of conflict, in which cricket comes under pressure from outside forces, has a very long history. The first problems of note involved clashes with Sunday observance, followed quickly by troubles over the illegal gambling which gained cricket an unsavoury reputation.

Throughout the last hundred years, the conflict between cricket's administrators and the cricketers themselves has bubbled. The problems of Yorkshire are very much in the news today, but the Great Australian Row between the Board of Control and the 1912 cricketers was just as sharp in its day, as was the Nottinghamshire strike of 1881.

The Packer Affair brought financial considerations once more to the surface, but to a greater or lesser extent these are bound to be a part of any professional activity and thus touch cricket as much as any walk of life.

The only conflict in the game which is purely of its own making is that connected with the Laws. Like the other aspects, it has recurred with regularity when the batsman has become too dominant. The Bodyline episode was a typical example and no doubt there will be other ideas, as yet undeveloped, to curb high scoring.

Let those who will, remember only the sunny days, but without the rain cricket would not hold the same fascination.

Peter Wynne-Thomas
Peter Arnold

January 1984

1 Early Skirmishes

Cricket in some form had been played for perhaps three hundred years before the first report of a conflict with the authorities, the Protestant church. The most famous of the early brushes with ecclesiastical hierarchy occurred at Boxgrove in 1722:

> Boxgrove, I present Raphe West, Edward Hartley, Richard Slaughter, William Martin, Richard Martin junior together with others in their company whose names I have no notice of for playing at cricket in the churchyard on Sunday the fifth of May after sufficient warning to the contrary, for three special reasons: first for that is contrary to the 7th article secondly for that they use to breake the church-windows with the ball and thirdly for that a little childe had like to have her braines beaten out with a cricket batt.

The Accounts of the Churchwarden and Overseers for the parish of Eltham reveal another example of cricketers falling foul of these protectors of the Lord's Day:

This year 1654	*An account of all such moneys as hath been recyved for misdemenrs of whome & howe disposed of*	
Cricket players on ye Lords Day	*Recd of Francis Clayford*	*2s*
	Edw Layton	*2s*
	John Poole	*2s*
	Will Foxe	*2s*
	Will Starbrock	*2s*
	Widd Roodes sonne	*2s*

Much more dramatic is the pamphlet which tells of the dire consequences resulting from the sin of Sunday cricket:

The Sabbath Breakers; Or, Young-Man's Dreadful Warning Piece. Being a very dismal Account of four Young-Men, who made a Match to Play at Cricket, on Sunday the 6th of this instant July, 1712, in a Meadow near Maiden Head Thicket; and as they were at Play, there rode out of the Ground, a Man in Black with a Cloven-Foot, which put them in great consternation; but as they stood in this Frighted Condition, the Devil flew up in the Air, in a Dark Cloud with Flames of Fire, and in his Room he lete a very Beautiful Woman, and Robert Yates and Richard Moore hastily stepping up to her, being charmed with her Beauty went to kiss her, but in attempt they instantly fell down Dead.

The other two Simon Jackson and George Grantham seeing this Tragical Sight, ran home to Maiden Head, where they now lye in a Distracted Condition.

Also the Minister at Maiden Head Pray'd with them frequently his Prayer is here at Large and likewise his Sermon which he preach'd the Sunday following, the Text is Remember the Sabbath Day to Keep it Holy. Exod. 20 Ver 80.

Prosecution for playing cricket on Sunday was by no means confined to the 17th and 18th centuries. In 1843 a member of Parliament drew the attention of the Attorney-General to the fact that six boys had been fined, with costs, fifteen shillings each for playing cricket on Sunday and if some local patron of the game had not come forward to pay these fines, the boys would have been in serious trouble. The Attorney-General ruled that the conviction was illegal if the boys had been playing in their own parish.

The clergy themselves were split on the subject. Some quite noted cricketers gave up the game immediately on being ordained. The Rev E. T. Drake, who played three times for Cambridge University against Oxford and was regarded as one of the best all-rounders of his day, more or less retired from important matches because his bishop frowned upon his clergy-men being involved in anything which was tainted by gambling. A few men of the cloth took the precaution of playing under an alias – the Rev J. Dolphin played for Norfolk in 1831 under the name J. Copford. The Rev Henry Venn, a few days before he was ordained, made, according to his biographer, a very dramatic gesture:

> When the game terminated in favour of the side on which he played, he threw down his bat, saying, 'Whoever wants a bat that has done me good service may take that, as I have no further occasion for it.' His friends inquiring the reason, he replied 'Because I am to be ordained on Sunday and I will never have it said of me "Well struck, Parson!" '. . . He could never be persuaded to play any more.

The church therefore came into conflict with cricket on two counts. The first, which upset the narrow Puritan sects, was the playing of games on Sunday. By and large this problem was, although spread throughout the British Isles, confined to particular bigotted communities and at least in the 19th century was not a major factor affecting cricket, rather a minor irritant.

The second count was the association of clergymen and 'decent folk' with the low life of gamblers surrounding any enterprise which apparently allows people to make easy money, or in most cases lose it!

In addition many cricket clubs, perhaps the vast majority, had their headquarters in taverns, and beerhouses. The connection of cricket and drink initially made many of the 19th century Temperance organisations fight shy of the game, but soon it was realised that the way to persuade young cricketers out of the bars was for the Temperance movements to create their own cricket clubs based on the Church Hall or the local chapel. A prime example of this is found in one of the most famous of Nottingham's old clubs – Forest Wanderers. The side began life in 1875 as Bloomsgrove Sunday School CC, being run by Radford Congregationalists from their Mission Hall in Radford. Simultaneously, the Church of England founded a team in the same parish -- Christ Church CC.

Cricket on Sundays was frowned upon well into the 20th century. Between the wars some club sides would play under a different title on Sundays in order not to offend their stricter patrons, but the Second World War brought a general acceptance of Sunday cricket, and the religious stranglehold was broken when first-class County cricket took place on the Lord's Day for the first time in May 1966. It was illegal to charge money for admission, so the County authorities sold scorecards at inflated prices to get round this law. Financially, the move to Sunday cricket was a great success and led to the advent of the John Player League in 1969. Although this happened only 15 years ago, it now seems part of the normal cricket programme. The County Clubs, however, were at first cautious in the extreme. A typical Committee Report of 1965 notes:

> Following the decision by the Advisory CCC to permit Sunday cricket on an experimental basis, your Committee have arranged two such fixtures in the coming season. The decision to do so was only taken after the fullest deliberation for the Committee are well aware of, and fully respect, the views of a number of members who are opposed to this. But it cannot be emphasised too strongly that this is an experiment only; payment in the normal way at the gate will, of course, not be demanded. In no case will Sunday play begin prior to 2.00 pm, so that those wishing to attend a Church Service and an afternoon's cricket may do both.

In Australia the ban on first-class Sunday cricket collapsed in 1964–65, thus preceding England. In those countries which were predominantly non-Christian, notably India and Pakistan, cricket had long been played on Sundays though some English cricketers declined to take part, notably Jack Hobbs in 1930–31. More recently, Vic Pollard of New Zealand refused to play in Test Matches which included a Sunday.

For most of the 18th Century we are indebted to newspapers as the source of the vast majority of the details concerning cricket – the first printed matchcard appeared in 1776 and the first Annual in 1791. The earliest instructional book on the game was not to appear until the following century. The early newspaper reports are not concerned with the cricket scores and certainly not the prowess of the individual players. They are interested primarily in the amount of money at stake. Finance, therefore, enters into cricket in its infancy and the myth that monetary considerations have only recently begun to overwhelm the 'amateur spirit' embodied in such Byronic phrases as 'Join'd together in cricket's manly toil' is nothing more than wishful thinking.

In 1718 Kent played London for half a guinea a man and when it looked as if Kent would lose, three of their team left to avoid having to pay and the affair was only settled by an expensive lawsuit:

> On Monday the first inst. was played a famous game of Cricket in the White Conduit Fields at Islington by eleven London gamesters against eleven Kentish gamesters who call themselves the Punch Club Society, for half a guinea a man. After a trial of their skill, which lasted about four hours, the Kentish men, whether it was for want of their celestial liquor (punch) to cheer up their exhausted spirits, I cannot determine; but be that as it will, they thought they would be worsted and therefore to the surprise of a numerous crowd of spectators, three of their men made an elopement, and got off the ground without going in, and made the best of their (way) home, hoping thereby to save their money; but we hear the London gamesters are resolved not to be bubbled in that manner, and are therefore determined to commence a suit at law against them to oblige them to pay their money.

Justice was done, as the following report shows:

> The great cricket match betwixt the Londoners and the Kentish men, for which there has been a famous trial at law; and by a rule of the court was ordered to be played out, in which the Kentish men had four men to play, and to get 30 to come up with the Londoners, was played in White-Conduit-Fields near Islington. The Kentish men were bowled out after they had got 9 and lost the match. 'Tis reckoned the law-suit will amount to £200. The match was played for a guinea a man each side.

The sums for which the teams played increased quite alarmingly. In the 1720s, 100, even 200, guineas was often put up by the backers of the two sides. Crowds watching the games now numbered thousands and betting during the game became common with the odds constantly altering as the teams' fortunes ebbed and flowed. A typical report in 1735 of a match between London and Surrey reads:

> As soon as the wickets were pitched, 6 to 4 was offered on the county side. The Londoners went in first, and got 22 notches before ever a one was out. Then the odds were 6 to 4 on London, who got 67 notches the first innings. Then the county went in and headed the Londoners about 30 notches, upon which there was 4 to 1 on the county. Upon London's second innings, four of them were put out before they headed the county; the bets were then a guinea to half-a-crown. Afterwards London headed the county 42 notches before they went out. The second innings of the county, the first four were out for 10 notches, which reduced the bets equal, and so continued till the time agreed upon was expired, when two hands were to come in and 9 notches to tie.

The match was a return of a game played in May; Surrey lost that first encounter and a preview of the second notes: 'The three or four bunglers who played on the Surrey side at Moulsey Hurst last Saturday do not play!' This second game took place on the Artillery Ground, Moorgate, cricket's principal venue for many years. As such it built up a most unsavoury reputation for collecting together large crowds of undesirables. In 1731 the Surrey v Sussex match, which was attended by 'many thousand spectators, of whom a great number were persons of distinction, of both sexes, ended with the mob attacking the Surrey team and tearing the shirts from their backs.'

The reason for this seems to have been that the Surrey team arrived late and in consequence the match had to be left drawn. When time was called Sussex only required a few to win with four or five wickets to fall and thus the bets were not paid out. A law suit was threatened to force the teams to complete the match, but the suit seems to have come to nothing. The Surrey team generally gained a rather disreputable image and in 1734 actually 'having been regaled with a good dinner etc., gratis, withdrew (from a match with London) and have not since been heard of . . .'

In the 1730s the sums had risen to £1,000 a side, staked by the Duke of Richmond and other patrons -- the crowds grew steadily as did the confusion: 'There was a surprising multitude of people present and a great deal of mischief was done, by some falling from their horses, others being rode over, etc., and one man was carried off for dead . . .'

The gambling fraternity were by now very much in control as this report makes clear:

A famous match of cricket was played between two famous Richmond men who have beaten all they have played against, being esteemed the best two in England, played on Kennington Common, against Mr. Wakeland the distiller, and Mr. George Oldner (whom they beat before at single-wicket), when a ball coming about breast high to one of the Richmond men, he struck at it and hit it up against the side of his nose, broke it, hurt his eye, and bruised his face in a most sad manner, and lost a great quantity of blood; yet notwithstanding this accident, some human brutes who laid against the Richmond men, insisted that he should play on (the Londoners being then ahead) or lose the match; upon which the Richmond man, after his nose was set and his face dressed and one side tied up, attempted to play again, when his nose fell a-bleeding afresh in a violent manner, that he was forced to throw up his bat; and the match to be played again in a fortnight.

A death occurred from violence in 1737:

John Smith, a mechanic, for many years foreman to Mr. Strong, a painter in Doctors Commons, died of a wound he received by a cut from a stone yesterday at the cricket-match on Kennington Common, when the mob outrageously threw dirt, dung etc, on account of the people entering the line.

A writer in the *Gentleman's Magazine* of September 1743 is in no doubt as to the bad influence of the game on the population:

In diversions as well as business, circumstances alter things mightily, and what in one man may be decent, may in another be ridiculous; what is innocent in one light may be quite the contrary in another; neither is it at all impossible that exercise may be strained too far. A journeyman shoemaker may play from five o-clock on Saturday in the afternoon till it is dark at skittles, provided he has worked all the rest of the week. Yet I can't say but it would shock me a little if I saw honest Crispin tipping against a member of either House of Parliament. All diversions at exercises have certain bounds as to expense, and when they exceed this it is an evil in itself and justly liable to censure. Upon what reasons are all the laws against gaming founded? Are not these the chief – that they break in upon business, expose people to great dangers, and cherish a spirit of covetousness, in a way directly opposed to industry? The most wholesome exercise and the most innocent diversion may change its nature entirely if people, for the sake of gratifying their humour, keep unfit company. I have been led into these reflections, which are certainly just in themselves, by some odd stories I have heard of cricket matches, which I own, however, to be so strange and incredible that, if I had not received them from eye-witnesses, I could never have yielded to them any belief. Is it not a very wild thing to be as serious in making such a match as in the most material occurrences in life? Would it not be extremely odd to see lords and gentlemen, clergymen and lawyers, associating themselves with butchers and cobblers in pursuit of their diversions? or can there be anything more absurd than making such matches, for the sake of profit, which is to be shared amoungst people so remote in their quality and circumstances? Cricket is certainly a very innocent and wholesome exercise, yet it may be abused if either great or little people make it their business. It is grossly abused when it is made the subject of public advertisements, to draw together great crowds of people who ought all of them to be somewhere else. Noblemen, gentlemen and clergymen have certainly a right to divert themselves in what manner they think fit; nor do I dispute their privilege of making butchers, cobblers, or tinkers their companions, provided they are gratified to keep them company. But I very much doubt whether they have any right to invite thousands of people to be spectators of their agility at the expense of their duty and honesty. The time of people of fashion may be, indeed, of very little value, but in a trading country the time of the meanest man ought to be of some worth to himself and to the community. The diversion of cricket may be proper in holiday time and in the country; but, upon days when men ought to be busy, and in the neighbourhood of a great city, it is not only improper but mischievous to a high degree. It draws numbers of people from their employments to the ruin of their families. It brings together crowds of apprentices and servants, whose time is not their own. It propagates a spirit of idleness at a juncture when, with the utmost industry, our debts, taxes and decay of trade will scarce allow us to get bread. It is a most notorious breach of the laws, as it gives the most open encouragement to gaming – the advertisements most impudently reciting that great sums are laid, so that some people are so little ashamed of breaking the laws they had a hand in making that they give public notice of it.

After 1770 there was a definite attempt to stop cricket as public entertainment on the Artillery Ground:

The game of Cricket which requires the utmost exertion of strength and agility, was followed until of late years, for manly exercise, animated by a noble spirit of Emulation. This sport has too long been perverted from diversion and innocent pastime to excessive gaming and public dissipation: Cricket matches are now degenerated into business of importance. The increasing evil our magistracy ought to suppress in the Artillery Ground. It is confidently said, that a set of idle fellows, or more properly a gang of dextrous gamblers, are hired and maintained by a most noble lord, at so little expense as £1,000 a year.

The great days of the Artillery Ground were finally ending and for a decade and more, most of the important matches were staged outside London, notably by the Committee of the Hambledon Club.

Although matches were still played for a certain sum and bookmakers were in evidence the scale was much reduced. It was however a long time before the game became 'respectable' – when in 1794 some pupils of Charterhouse and Westminster organised a match between the two schools, the game was played under the title 'City of London v City of Westminster' and in 1796 the headmaster of Eton flogged the entire team that played Westminster in defiance of his orders.

The wounds inflicted upon the game by the backers of the various major teams and the associated bookmakers and gambling set healed themselves with the passage of time mainly due to the economic change resulting from the Napoleonic Wars. The final hiccup occurred in 1817 when the leading professional cricketer of the day, William Lambert, was accused of selling a match and banned from Lord's for life. At about the same time the remaining bookmakers were ejected from the enclosure at Lord's, though matches elsewhere still drew the betting fraternity:

> Play commenced about two o-clock on Monday with betting 5 to 4 against Bury, who took first innings. During the progress of this innings, a man or two being out for a few notches, the odds rather increased, but Bury having made up 76, they reverted to what they were at starting. Thus the game stood on Monday evening. On the following morning play resumed about eleven by the Nottingham side taking their innings; when four or five good men were soon out for a few runs the betting was in favour of Bury as much as 3 to 2 and so it remained till the close of their innings . . .

This report from the *Bury and Norwich Post* of 21 September 1825 continues in the same vein for a column and more and plainly demonstrates that the gambling aspect remained for many the most important factor of the contest.

For a hundred years the major cricketing fixtures had been arranged by a handful of wealthy promoters, financing their own teams. These promoters employed cricketers on their estates as grooms, gardeners and the like, but gradually the wealthy patrons gave way to groups of gentlemen, who formed Clubs to run cricket teams. The first major example was the Hambledon Club, to be followed by the Marylebone Club and other lesser Clubs. These Clubs employed cricketers for the season and used these professionals both as practice bowlers and to reinforce the Club Team. In some cases the Club team consists almost entirely of professionals and in others only the Gentlemen members of the Club, but generally it consisted of a mixture of the two. Whatever the composition of the Club team, the Committee of the Club's subscribers controlled all the cricketing activities and the payment of the Club professionals. In 1846 however, the leading professionals, seeing that they could make much more money by promoting and running matches without the help of wealthy patrons or Clubs took matters into their own hands and almost overnight changed the face of cricket, as a public spectacle, throughout England.

The instigator of this revolution was William Clarke, who banded together the top cricketers of the day and formed the 'England Eleven,' prepared to play matches against any opposition anywhere in the British Isles provided the England Eleven was guaranteed a minimum sum, any profits over and above that sum being split between the Eleven and whoever provided the ground and the opposition team. The public flocked to the matches and the England Eleven became, if anything, too successful. Clarke, as the Manager, kept most of the profits for himself.

William Caffyn, a member of the England Eleven, noted in his memoirs:

> There had long been dissatisfaction among some of the Players against Clarke. It was thought that Clarke was coining money, and that they ought to be better paid. I believe Wisden at the time put the matter straight to Clarke, who answered him somewhat roughly, and caused a breach between them.

Wisden – later to found the famous *Cricketers' Almanack* – left the England Eleven at the close of the 1851 season and the following year became the coach at Harrow School. When the school term ended he created his own professional Eleven – the United All England Eleven – which Clarke saw as a counter-attraction to the England Eleven. After a game at Portsmouth, Wisden took his side to Newmarket and here a meeting took place between Clarke and Wisden at which Clarke unsuccessfully tried to persuade Wisden to give up his promotion of a rival eleven. The meeting proved to be a total failure and the two parties were now completely at loggerheads. Wisden's side issued the following statement:

> At a meeting held at the Adelphi Hotel, Sheffield, this 7th day of September 1852, by the members of the United Eleven of England, it was unanimously resolved, – That neither the members of the above Eleven shall at any time play in any match of cricket, for or against, wherein William Clarke may have the management or control (county matches excepted), in consequence of the treatment they have received from him at Newmarket and elsewhere.

What this meant in cricketing terms was that the best 30 professional cricketers in England were now divided into two camps and would have nothing to do with each other – county matches were exempt, but in 1853 there were only four major inter-county contests, so this clause was hardly worth noting.

The situation in 1853 was almost an exact parallel to the split between the leading Australian cricketers caused by Kerry Packer in 1978. Neither side would move from its entrenched position and since both were able to arrange enough fixtures to remain financially successful the split continued until Clarke's death in August 1856. The emnity between the two professional elevens died with Clarke and the following year saw the England Eleven play against the United Eleven at Lord's before what was described as the biggest crowd ever to attend a match on that ground.

The reconciliation between the leading professionals was destined to last only a few seasons. Ill-feeling seems to have begun again in 1861 when Spiers and Ponds, the catering firm, decided to organise the tour of Australia by the English professionals. The Northern players refused to go, demanding more money, but the Southern players, mainly those of Surrey, agreed to the terms offered. According to some sources the fact that the captaincy was offered to Stephenson of Surrey, rather than Parr of Notts, was another bone of contention.

In 1862, the discontent flared up once more during the England v Surrey match at the Oval. England hit the then colossal score of 503, and when Surrey began their reply, the umpire, John Lillywhite no-balled Willsher, the main England bowler, for 'throwing'. The England side walked off the field and refused to continue the match until Lillywhite was dismissed and another umpire appointed. The England side claimed that Lillywhite was acting under the instructions of the Surrey Club. Caffyn, the Surrey player, who went to Australia as a coach in the 1860s, notes in his memoirs: 'The no-balling caused a lot of unpleasantness for a long time afterwards; some of the Northern players becoming bitterly prejudiced against Surrey and the Oval.'

The Notts team refused to play Surrey the following year and though the match was resumed a year later – Notts and Surrey were the two strongest counties in England – the Notts captain, Parr, would not play against Surrey. In 1865 the animosity broke out again when the 9th Surrey wicket fell with 14 needed to win and Sewell, the last batsman, was run out by a yard and a half, but given 'not out'. Haygarth notes: 'This match was not resumed in 1866, the old grievance having been re-opened, and the Nottingham players and spectators being greatly dis-satisfied with a decision of the umpire towards the conclusion of the match.' The Yorkshire players were just as opposed to Surrey as the Notts ones, no doubt egged on by Parr and perhaps 'blackmailed' by the fact Parr controlled the England Eleven in which the Yorkshiremen played. In the Yorkshire v Surrey match earlier in the season it was noted:

> Five of the Yorkshire players refused (for reasons best known to themselves) to assist their County. Their names were G. Atkinson, G. Anderson, R. Iddison, J. Rowbotham and E. Stephenson, but the Sheffield Committee wisely determined to play the match with the best men they could get . . .

'The reasons best known to themselves' had come about during the course of the 1864 season. A North v South match had been arranged to be played on the Middlesex County Ground, Islington on 5, 6 and 7 September. The match was under the auspices of the United All England Eleven and Roger Iddison, a member of both the Yorkshire team and the United, was to select and captain the North. Iddison either would not or could not persuade the best Northern players to come and did not come himself, saying he would send his brother (almost a nonentity) – even his brother did not arrive and the match was a farce, the South winning by an innings. The Southern players retaliated by refusing to appear in the next North v South match arranged for Newmarket on 6, 7 and 8 October. In November the seven leading Southern players in the United All England Eleven then announced they were resigning and a week later founded the 'United South of England Eleven'. *The Sporting Life* noted: 'The mischief, as our readers are aware, has long been brewing, and various causes, into which we shall not enter, have from time to time widened the breach between the North and South men.'

The principal match at Lord's since 1857 had been, from the public's viewpoint, the England v United All England fixture. As a result of the latest schism there were now virtually no Southern players in either side. The two Elevens played however, at Lord's in May 1866, but refused to appear with any of the Southern players in either the Gentlemen v Players match or North v South match – the latter game was therefore meaningless, the North being dismissed for 95 and 65 and the game being over at lunch-time on the second morning.

The split between North and South became virtually complete in 1867 when the England v United All England match was moved to Manchester – over the years the match had been played for the Cricketers' Benefit Fund and this continued to be the case in 1867. The MCC, who from the 1790s were the arbiters of the Laws, reacted with the following statement:

> Taking into consideration the conduct of certain of the professionals of England during the season of 1866, it is no longer desirable to extend the patronage of the Marylebone Club to the Cricketers' Fund exclusively; but a fund has now been formed which shall be called 'The Marylebone Professional Fund' which shall have for its object the support of professional players who, during their career, shall have conducted themselves to the entire satisfaction of the Committee of the MCC.

The bitterness went on through 1867. When the Yorkshire Committee organised their annual fixture v Surrey at Bramall Lane, the leading Yorkshire professionals, as in the previous years, refused to appear, but the Cambridgeshire professionals this year sided with the dissidents, and because the Yorkshire Committee had played the match with Surrey, the Cambridge side refused to fulfil the Yorkshire v Cambridgeshire fixture due to be staged at Bramall Lane a fortnight later. A report noted that the Cambridgeshire professionals would not come 'out of spite'. The dissident Yorkshire and Cambridgeshire players then arranged a fixture at Bradford among themselves, ignoring the Yorkshire County Committee. These wrangles and petty disputes meant that inter-County cricket in 1867 was pointless, if the object were to try to decide a Champion Country.

Season 1868 was little better. The Grand Whitsuntide match at Lord's – England v MCC – scarcely lived up to its title since the England Eleven played the United All England Eleven at Dewsbury on the same dates; again the North v South match at Lord's was a farce since the Northern professionals wouldn't come. The Gentlemen beat the Players both at Lord's and the Oval, mainly because the Northerners were absent. Notts resumed their fixture with Surrey, but the Notts captain, Parr, was conspicious by his absence.

The United All England Eleven folded up in 1869 and with its departure the Northern professionals 'now finding it to their advantage' began to re-appear at Lord's and the Oval – the rancour which had simmered for nearly a decade was at last ended, though there can be no doubt that the sharp rivalry which still exists between North and South to a large extent stemmed from the disputes of the 1860s.

2 The Nottinghamshire Strike

After the troubles – or in the case of the MCC during the troubles – of the 1860s, the Committees of the major Clubs began the task of bringing their unruly professionals to heel. Only Cambridgeshire failed. That County had three self-willed top professionals in Tom Hayward, Bob Carpenter and George Tarrant. Aside from them the County was rather weak, with very little in the way of strong amateur support either on the field or financially. The stage was reached when all three would play for the County only if they were captain and this seems to have been the final blow.

The public had tired of the exhibition matches promoted by the England Eleven and its off-spring. These games in the 1870s created interest only in the locality in which they were played, and the public were now keen to see inter-county cricket and to identify themselves with their own County side. This partisanship strengthened the hand of the County Committees and the occasional professional who stepped out of line quickly found himself out of the County side and out of pocket.

Since 1861, England teams had been visiting Australia regularly and several English professionals had stayed in Australia to coach the local players. In March 1877 came the celebrated victory of the Australians over the English tourists at Melbourne (the first Test match). The following year the Australians came to England for the first time as a national team (the Aborigines had toured in 1868).

The 1878 tour was a huge success, the Australian team being greeted by large crowds everywhere they travelled. Haygarth noted at the end of the visit: 'This was Australia's last match in England, and, as everywhere, the crowds to see them play were enormous; so were their profits also.' It was the final phrase which caused unease and was eventually to lead to the Great Strike.

The money made by the tourists raised two separate issues amongst English cricketers. One was the 'status' of the Australians. Were they Gentlemen or were they Players? The contemporary scorebooks neatly sit on the fence – 'Mr W. L. Murdoch' is the description used, whereas the Englishmen in the same match are either 'W. W. Read Esq.' or 'J. Smith'.

The problem was not simply one of the correct form of address. In 1878 there was a great divide between Gentlemen and Players – the two classes used different hotels, different railway carriages, different dressing-rooms, different dining-rooms and, in the more select pavilions, different entrances and exits to and from the field of play.

The advent of the Australians, however, acted only as a catalyst in bringing to the surface troubles that had been brewing since the emergence of the Gloucestershire Club early in the same decade. The Gloucester County side consisted of eleven Gentlemen – not a professional in its ranks – yet when the Western County played England at the Oval in 1878, the visitors presented the Surrey Committee with a bill which was higher than it would have been if the Gloucester team had been solely composed of professionals. *The Sportsman* commented:

> The original cause of the dispute was the refusal of the committee of the Surrey County Club to pay a sum of £102.10s presented by the Gloucestershire secretary as the bill of expenses for his eleven in the match between Gloucestershire and England, played at the Oval in August last. Such an amount would generally be considered most excessive even for a county eleven, composed entirely or almost exclusively of professionals, and no-one will blame the executive at the Oval for their practical protest against the payment of what may fairly be described as an exorbitant demand for a team professedly constituted of amateur cricketers. The Gloucestershire committee, deeming the objection of the Surrey executive justified, reduced the expenses claimed to £80.10s., and this settlement, it might have been expected,

would have brought a not very savoury transaction to a close. But there were other issues involved, and the Gloucestershire amateurs deemed it necessary in defence of their reputation, to continue the discussion on broader grounds.

The issue was brought before the Gloucestershire Committee and the Chairman of the Committee, when it came to a vote, refused to allow Dr E. M. Grace to register his opinion on the grounds that he was an interested party (E. M. Grace's expenses for the match in question were £20.00, twice the sum usually allowed for the highest paid professional!)

The dispute rumbled on with a series of bitter letters appearing in the press. The Gloucestershire Club then unanimously passed the following new rule: 'That only actual expenses shall be paid to members playing for the county, except where special arrangements are made, such arrangements to be made from time to time by the committee.' Just the type of rule to please everybody and nobody. *Lillywhite's Cricketers' Companion* commented on the 1878 season:

The question of the relative status of Amateur and Professional cricketers has been debated for some seasons past, and we have on several occasions stated in plain terms that the Marylebone Club should long since have nipped in the bud an evil which was patent to all but those who were wilfully blind. In dealing with a question involving the interests of an entire community, no dread of treading on a single individual's corns should have hindered the one acknowledged legislative body from doing its duty. The Note issued by the MCC at the close of last season should have been issued four or five seasons ago, but cricketers must be thankful that the leading club has, however late in the day, recognised an evil which has been injuring the best interests of the game for some seasons past. It is satisfactory to learn at last that 'no cricketer who takes more than his expenses in any match shall be qualified to play for the Gentlemen against the Players at Lord's' but it is somewhat surprising to read the assertion appended to the Note that 'This rule has been invariably adhered to by the Marylebone Club since the management of the finances of the Club has been in its own hands' for ninety-nine of every hundred cricketers know as well as we do that this statement is, to use a mild term, hardly consistent with facts. One well-known cricketer in particular, has not been an absentee from the Gentlemen's eleven at Lord's for many years past, and that he has made larger profits by playing cricket than any Professional ever made, is an acknowledged fact. How the Marylebone Club can reconcile their statement with this fact, even with any reasonable amount of word-twisting, we are unable to conceive. However the matter is not actionable, and may be left to the consciences of the framers of the Note.

The cricketer to which Lillywhite refers was W. G. Grace, and the major problem here was that the presence of Grace at a match added literally hundreds of pounds to the gate. It was therefore hardly surprising that the various County Committees, as well as the MCC, ignored the letter of the law when it came to paying W. G. Grace his 'expenses'.

Meanwhile, the Australians, who on their 1878 tour, demanded 80 per cent of the gate money, further complicated the division between the two classes of cricketers. They annoyed the supporters of the 'true amateur' traditions, but the second, and in the long term, worse problem, was that they all made much more money than the English professionals.

Because of the great success of the Australians, Surrey lent their ground free of charge for a match between the touring side and a team selected by James Lillywhite, the game to be considered the equal of the England *v* Australia match at Melbourne in March 1877. The major English professionals refused to take part in the contest because they were only offered £10 each, whereas when a similar match had taken place in Australia, the English tourists had paid the Australians £20 per man. The advertisements for the game, however, still carried the names of the leading English professionals. As a result the following letter appeared in *The Sporting Life*:

> Sir – Having observed at the Oval, that we are announced to play against the Australians there on Monday, Tuesday and Wednesday September 2nd, 3rd and 4th, we wish, through your columns, to inform the public, so that they may

not be misled, that we are not engaged at all in the match and do not intend to play. We also beg to inform the public that it is not the intention of any of the recognised Yorkshire players to take part in the match. If, Sir, any letters may be addressed to you on the subject of our terms of remuneration, we beg to inform the public that we only asked for what we paid the Australians in our benefit match in the Antipodes. Signed – W. Oscroft, J. Selby, F. Morley, A. Shrewsbury, A. Shaw, W. Barnes, H. Jupp, E. Pooley and W. Flowers.'

The players named consisted of seven Notts professionals and two Surrey ones. The whole question of amateur status and of payment lay dormant in 1879, but when the Australian 'amateurs' decided to arrange a second tour to England in 1880 and a very inferior fixture list was cobbled together, solely with the object of making money, the critics had another field day. *Lillywhite's Cricketers' Annual* was outspoken on the subject:

> The visit of the Australians nearly produced a permanent rupture between the cricketers of the old and the new world, which might even probably have in some small measure affected the political relations of the two countries. For ourselves, we claim to have been ardent admirers of the cricket shown by these Antipodean players, but at the same time we must admit that their visit, for many reasons, was ill-advised. The recollections of the commercial spirit, which had inspired the first team, were still disagreeably fresh in the minds of Englishmen, and this sudden appearance of a second party, was suggestive of a trading concern, whereby Colonial players might systematically make these trips a matter of personal speculation. It was urged too very properly, that to recognise the Australian team as amateurs, when they notoriously made money out of these tours, was tacitly to violate the recent enactment of the Marylebone Club defining an amateur, and this anomalous position of the Colonials was a real stumbling block, a point that will have to be settled before another eleven leaves the Colonies.

The other Lillywhite publication, the *Cricketers' Companion* made the point:

If the Australians did not make cricket their profession in their native land, they most decidedly did when they came to this country: for all who had anything to do with them soon found out how keen they were about £.s.d. I do not blame them for that; but by doing so they lost all claim to be considered amateurs. Our professionals, when they visit the Colonies, were well paid, but they went out as professionals. Lord Harris's Eleven [1878/9] with the exceptions of Emmett and Ulyett, went out as amateurs, and were treated as such.

The 1880 Australians in fact almost took over the role formerly played by the England and the United All England Elevens, nearly all their matches being against local Eighteens, and in the months of May, June, July and August, only a total of five matches were contested against County sides. The Australians were patently a much bigger draw than the remnants of the old professional English touring sides and this meant not only a final nail in the English sides' coffin but that the English professionals lost a useful source of income, which further added to their grievances. In August 1880 several of the County Committees, seeing the great success the Australians were making of their tour, tried to organise a fixture with the visitors during September. The Australians were by now well aware of their value. Nottinghamshire were among the counties to approach the Australian management and the tenor of the negotiations can be gleaned from the note which appeared in the *Nottingham Guardian* on 11 September:

> A second attempt has been made by the Notts County Executive to arrange a match between the County Eleven and the Australians on the Trent Bridge ground, but the same reason which before put an end to the negotiations – the question of terms – will again in all probability act as an effective barrier to this very interesting match taking place. The matter however is not definitely settled.

The Notts Committee did in fact agree terms with the Australians, and the match was to commence on 23 September. The Notts Secretary, Captain Holden, immediately wrote to Alfred

Shaw, the leading Notts bowler, who was at Bradford, where he and six other Notts players were appearing for the Players of the North v Australians in a game organised by Shaw for the Bradford Committee. Captain Holden wrote:

> Sir – I am directed by the Committee to ask you and the following, viz: W. Barnes, F. Morley, W. Oscroft, W. H. Scotton, J. Selby and A. Shrewsbury to play for the County against the Australians in a match commencing September 23rd. The terms are, in which Daft [the Notts captain] fully agrees, that the Australians are to have half the receipts, the remaining half, after paying expenses, to be divided between the Eleven and the County Club.

Shaw wrote back by return to say that he, together with Selby, Morley, Shrewsbury, Barnes and Scotton, required a guaranteed £20 per man. The Notts Committee, having erected a number of temporary stands and advertised the match, could only comply with the demands of the players, though under protest. Directly the match was over, the following letter appeared in the press:

> Sir: At a meeting of the committee of the Notts County Cricket Club held this day [30 September], I was directed to forward the following correspondence for publication. I think it right to mention that it was decided to pay the four players who did not make the demand, £21 each. Signed – Hy Holden, Hon Sec, Notts CCC. [The letters between the club and Alfred Shaw were then published].

During the winter of 1880/81 Shaw, having made a success of the match he organised with the Australians at Bradford in 1880, began the arrangements for a match between Nottinghamshire and Yorkshire on the same ground for July, 1881. The Nottinghamshire Secretary, Captain Holden, wrote to Shaw on 9 February objecting to him arranging a County match without the sanction of the County Committee. Shaw wrote back stating that Richard Daft, the then Nottinghamshire captain, had arranged a similar fixture in 1873 without any objections being raised by the Nottinghamshire Committee. Shaw and his partner, Shrewsbury, were invited to meet the

Nottinghamshire Committee on 23 April. The cricketers refused. A further invitation was issued for a meeting in the pavilion at Trent Bridge during the Eastertide Nottinghamshire Colts match. Shaw, Shrewsbury and Selby agreed to meet any three of the Committee, provided Captain Holden was not present. The Committee refused to accept this proviso.

It now became clear that the arrangement of the Nottinghamshire v Yorkshire match at Bradford was not the only irritant between the players and the Nottinghamshire Committee. Shaw stated that each of the leading Nottinghamshire professionals had been sent a letter in March asking if he would sign an agreement to play in any match for the county for which he was selected on the usual terms of £5 lose or draw and £6 for a win. A reply to the letter was required by 26 March.

The seven leading players – Shaw, Morley, Shrewsbury, Selby, Barnes, Scotton and Flowers – then issued a three point ultimatum to the Committee:

1. That the match between Nottinghamshire and Yorkshire at Bradford should be allowed to take place under that title.
2. That every player should be guaranteed a Benefit after 10 years.
3. That the seven players named above should be engaged by the County Club for all the County matches of 1881 and not on a match by match basis.

The Committee went so far as to agree to engage five of the players for all the matches – Scotton and Flowers being excluded. In an editorial the *Nottingham Guardian* thought that the Committee were not wise in conceding even this to the players, but the editorial went on to state that 'our troubles are due to the success of the Australian tourists'.

The first inter-county Notts match of 1881 was against Sussex at Trent Bridge on 26 May. The seven professionals played, but again refused to attend a meeting with the Committee. On 1 June, the newspapers announced that 'the differences between the Committee and the players had not been amicably settled' and the County would therefore be without the seven for their match against Lancashire commencing 2 June.

Alfred Shaw, who acted as the spokesman for the seven, claimed that Captain Denison, a leading member of the Nottinghamshire Committee, had accepted, on behalf of the Committee, the principle that all seven players should be engaged for the season, provided they apologise for not meeting the Committee when asked to do so. Shaw then said that they were willing to apologise, but he went on to say that this state of affairs would not have arisen in the days of Messrs. Johnson, Davy and Bromley (the three Nottinghamshire Secretaries who preceded Captain Holden in that office).

It now began to emerge that the real crux of the problem was the clash of personalities – the stubborn reactionary Captain Holden, who was not only the combined Honorary Secretary and Treasurer to the County Club, but also the Chief Constable of the County, and the equally hard-headed Alfred Shaw and Arthur Shrewsbury. Shaw was the best bowler in England – in 1880 he was the leading English bowler with 186 wickets, av. 8.54 – whilst Shrewsbury was regarded as the most promising of England's younger batsmen – he was to head the batting averages in 1885, 1886 and 1887.

The whole of the cricketing profession now watched this dispute, since the seven players involved were not merely seven ordinary county professionals, but seven of the top dozen professionals in England. All played Test cricket, and in 1880 Nottinghamshire had won the County Championship title with ease. In the preview of the 1881 season the following comment reflected opinion at the time: 'There are not a few who already are taking delight in balancing the County prospects for the ensuing season and almost universally the question to be solved is not exactly which shire to place first, but which to place second to Notts.'

Through June of 1881, the deadlock between the players and the Committee continued – the strikers held solid. On 19 July Captain Holden asked the MCC to mediate. Henry Perkins, the MCC Secretary, persuaded the seven players to agree to be available for selection for the next Nottinghamshire match. Captain Holden chose five of them, leaving out Shrewsbury and Flowers. The five chosen then refused to appear.

It was not until the first match of August that a break-through was finally achieved. Wilfred Flowers, the easiest-going of the seven strikers – *Wisden* noted in his obituary 'Modest about his achievements, quiet in manner and well-spoken, Flowers was generally popular and bore the "ups and downs" of life with much philosophy' – was the first of the seven to give way. He played against Gloucestershire and almost single-handed won the game for Nottinghamshire, taking 8 for 23 in the first innings. A week later Flowers was joined by Selby and Barnes in the match against Lancashire. Scotton and Morley played in the following game. Only Shrewsbury and Shaw stood out against the Committee for the whole season.

When the cricket annuals appeared, *Lillywhite's Cricketers' Annual* devoted a long article to the strike. The writer was certain where the intrinsic blame lay:

> The precise origin of the movement is difficult to trace, but indirectly the visits of the two Australian Elevens to England may be held responsible for the sudden and extraordinary change which took place in the bearing of professionals who had previously comported themselves most becomingly. The terms on which the Colonial Players were accepted over here were utterly false to men like Shaw, who knew that the home status of some was certainly not above the level of professional cricket in England, and here no doubt was the first sign of grievance. Then again, the readiness with which in many cases rather exorbitant demands of the Australian managers were met by some of our chief clubs probably had some influence in encouraging Alfred Shaw and Shrewsbury, who may be considered as the leaders of the movement, in believing that the withdrawal of the seven most capable members of the Eleven might reduce the management of a county even so rich in cricketers as Nottinghamshire to accede to the imposition of new stipulations in the recognised contracts.

Shaw and Shrewsbury both resumed their places in the County side the following year. The Nottinghamshire Minute Book noted on 13 May 1882: 'A. Shaw, J. Selby, W. Scotton and A. Shrewsbury apologize for their conduct in 1881 and are re-instated in the Eleven.' The bluff Captain Holden, whose lack of diplomacy was so much in evidence, resigned from his dual role as Secretary and Treasurer to the County Club at the end of the 1882 season. A series of blunders made his position untenable. The Australians returned for the third time in 1882 and arrived at Trent Bridge on 8 June to play Nottinghamshire. Australia batted first and collapsed to 41 for 5 by lunch. When the team came to get their refreshment, they found that Captain Holden had 'forgotten' to order a meal for them. The gallant captain, when rebuked for his negligence, replied that the Australians were amateurs and as such should provide their own lunches. This was no doubt the type of tactful remark, in the circumstances, that possibly provoked Shaw and Shrewsbury into action the year before. The Captain further confounded the tourists when their innings ended. Holden told the Australian captain that it was the Nottinghamshire secretary's prerogative to decide how long the roller should be used on the wickets between innings and had nothing to do with either the Australian captain or the umpires.

The next day some rude remarks regarding Holden were found to be chalked on the door of the hotel in which the Australian team were staying. Holden accused the Australian manager of writing the remarks. It was a rather rash accusation by a man who was Chief Constable and as it turned out totally without foundation – one of the camp-followers of the Australian party later admitted the 'crime'.

Even Holden could now see that he had little option but to resign and on 1 July he placed a letter of resignation on the table, though it did not take effect until the end of the year, as the man selected by the Committee to replace Holden declined.

A happier atmosphere was discernible at Trent Bridge, and the County Club, after being joint Champions with Lancashire in 1882, won the title outright in the four following seasons, under the leadership of Alfred Shaw.

The reputation that the Nottinghamshire professionals gained as 'hard men' was one which lingered on for many years and as late as 1935, Arthur Carr wrote in his autobiography of being offered the captaincy of the County in 1919:

Before I took over the captaincy busy people told me all sorts of disturbing things about the Nottinghamshire team and its players. For one thing, I was warned that they did not want 'any b—— amateurs' in the side and would set about getting me out of it. Well, all I can say is, that I have had nothing to complain about in my reception from the players.

Ironically, Carr was sacked, after 16 years as captain, because he championed the cause of Larwood and Voce against the Notts Committee – but that is a conflict which comes in another chapter.

3 Illegal Bowling

'That's throwing, not bowling!'
'There's nothing in the Laws against it.'

Batsman and bowler looked at the umpire. The umpire scratched his head. 'On the one hand,' he thought, 'if I side with the batsman, the bowler will walk off, but on the other, if I allow the bowler to continue, the batsman will leave.'

The elders, watching, pondered. 'It's not cricket, to bowl like that!'

The impetuous youths began to shout. Tempers rose along with voices. In a matter of moments a cricket field became a battle-field. The game was at an end. Nothing would be the same again.

Such a confrontation must have taken place not once but a dozen times in the early years of the eighteenth century, but the name of the man who finally convinced cricketers that the bowler could pitch the ball instead of bowling it along the ground is not recorded.

The concept of the pitched ball must have been the most dramatic development in the history of the game, because it changed the shape of both wicket and bat. Thus the revolution can hardly have been a peaceful affair, when it meant discarding the principal instruments of the game and manufacturing new ones. The traditionalists must have fought tooth and nail for the preservation of the status quo. Both batsman and bowler would need to evolve new techniques.

With no central authority controlling the Laws, and matches, in the main, only local affairs, the changeover was a gradual process. The progressives fought for their cause parish by parish, county by county. Between 1700 and 1740 the old hockey style bats were discarded for bats similar in shape to those used today. The wicket, which was originally wider than it was high, gave way to the upright version.

The earliest extant version of the Laws (1744) states:

> The bowler must deliver the Ball, with one foot behind the crease, even with the wicket; and when he has bowled one ball, or more, shall bowl to the Number of Four before he changes wicket, and he shall change but once in the same Innings.

There is clearly no mention of the method of delivery of the ball in this version of the Law. Neither is it mentioned in the 1727 Articles of Agreement drawn up by the Duke of Richmond and Mr Brodrick, which articles dwell upon contentious points that might arise in the matches being then proposed between teams collected by the two men. It is therefore very interesting to note the comments contained in some biographical notes concerning Thomas Walker, whose career with the famous Hambledon Club commenced about 1780:

> Never sure, was there such an unadulterated rustic. His figure was hard, with an ungain scrag of mutton frame, wilted applejohn face (he always looked 20 years older than he really was), long spider legs, as thick at the ankles as at the hips, and perfectly straight all the way down. A dry and rigid limbed chap, his skin was like the rind of an old oak, and as sapless. His knuckles were rarely knocked about by Harris's bowling (David used to say he liked to rind him), but he never showed blood. You might as well attempt to phlebotomize a mummy. He was also a very slow runner, and toiled like a tar on horseback, every member flying to the four winds. Noah Mann, who could go a great pace between wickets, often in a long hit caught Walker up, and patting him on the back said, 'You are rightly called Walker, for you never were a runner.' Walker had a thorough knowledge of the game, being also a foxheaded and crafty player. About two years after he joined Hambledon club, he began the system of jerking, or the round armed delivery. This owing to its

tremendous pace, was forbidden by a council of the Hambledon club [the then law givers], called on purpose.

The members of the Hambledon Club therefore permitted only underarm bowling, but it is a matter of opinion how far that Club's authority stretched, probably only to matches directly organised by the Club.

One can only assume that before a match took place, the backers of the two teams agreed as to whether or not to allow round-arm bowling. By the early years of the nineteenth century round-arm bowling was presumably relatively common. The *Sporting Magazine*, in reporting the England v Kent Match at Penenden Heath on 20, 21 and 22 July 1807 notes:

> In this match the straight-arm bowling introduced by John Willes Esq., was generally practised, and fully proved an obstacle in getting runs, in comparison to what might have been got by the straight forward bowling.

John Willes was born in Kent in 1777 and began playing in serious matches in the 1790s. The important phrase in the above comment is 'was generally practised'.

Despite the ruling of the Hambledon Club, which was made about 1785, when the MCC published a revised set of Laws in 1788, there was no note outlining 'round-arm' bowling, the bowling Law remaining almost exactly as it was in 1744.

The Laws published in 1809 by John Wallis of Newgate Street, London state:

> The Bowler shall deliver the ball with one foot behind the bowling-crease, and within the return-crease; and shall bowl four balls before he changes wickets, which he shall do but once in the same innings. He may order a striker at this wicket to stand on which side of it he pleases.'

Thus the Law regarding the bowler had scarcely altered since 1744. When however W. Lambert published his *Cricketers' Guide* in 1816 there was a fundamental change:

> The Bowler shall deliver the ball with one foot behind the bowling-crease, and within the return-crease, and shall bowl four balls before he changes wickets, which he shall do but

once in the same innings. If the bowler tosses the ball above the striker's head, or so wide that the striker cannot play at it, or out of the bounds of the bowling-crease, the party which is in shall be allowed one notch, to be put down to the byes, and such ball is not to be considered as one of the four balls. If 'No Ball' is called by the Umpire, the hitter may strike at it and get all the runs he can, and shall not be out except by running out. No more than two balls to be allowed at practice when a fresh bowler takes the ball before he proceeds. The bowler who gives the two balls is obliged to give four.

The ball must be delivered underhanded, not thrown or jerked, with the hand below the elbow at the time of delivering the ball. If the arm is extended straight from the body, or the back part of the hand be uppermost when the ball is delivered, or the hand horizontally extended, the Umpire shall call 'No Ball'.

The traditionalists must have finally forced the Law on the MCC and insisted that the clause regarding the height of the bowling arm be included. It is not known who was responsible for this change in the Law. Several authorities give the date as 1816, but this is merely based on the date in which Lambert issued his book. Because of what happened later one can assume that the new Law was enforced in matches involving the MCC.

John Willes persisted in his crusade, as the following notes in the *Morning Herald* make clear:

Mr. Willes and his bowling were frequently barred in making a match and he played sometimes amidst much uproar and confusion. Still he would persevere till the ring closed on the players, the stumps were lawlessly pulled up, and all came to a standstill.

So far as can be ascertained Willes did not play at Lord's from 1807 until 1822 when he was the organiser of the Kent team which met MCC on 15 and 16 July. Willes was determined to bring the matter to a head. MCC batted first and he opened the bowling only to be no-balled for throwing. Ashley Cooper's note in *Kent Cricket Matches* tells of the consequences:

When Mr. John Willes 'high' bowling in this match was stopped by Bentley (probably at the instigation of Lord F. Beauclerk) he threw down the ball in disgust, and jumping upon his horse, rode home and left all the players in the lurch. There were no railways in those days and it cost him £100 to take a team to London.

The no-balling of Willes caused no more than a temporary halt in the development of round-arm bowling. The conflict with MCC was resumed in earnest in 1826 by Sussex, who beat Kent twice and a combined Surrey and Hampshire team twice, with the aid of two bowlers who had recently adopted round-arm bowling, Jem Broadbridge and William Lillywhite. The former began to play about 1813, but it was not until the 1820s that he changed to medium pace round-arm bowling. Lillywhite was unknown to cricketing fame until he was 35. Later Haygarth noted:

> No cricketer ever came up to Lord's so late in life, commenced playing so old in great matches, and afterwards ran so long and brilliant a career lasting upwards of twenty seasons, and still bowling splendidly when nearly sixty years of age.

In 1827 Sussex challenged England in three matches and these games were regarded at the time as a challenge between the round-arm and under-arm bowling. In the first of the matches, played at Darnall, near Sheffield, Sussex won by 7 wickets, with Lillywhite and Broadbridge taking all the wickets which were attributed to bowlers. In the second match, at Lord's, the two round-arm bowlers were not quite so successful, but after the game the England players issued the following declaration:

> We, the undersigned, do agree that we will not play the third match between All England and Sussex, which is intended to be played at Brighton in July or August, unless the Sussex bowlers bowl fair – that is, abstain from throwing. (signed) T. Marsden, W. Ashby, W. Mathews, W. Searle, J. Saunders, T. C. Howard, W. Caldecourt, F. Pilch, T. Beagley.

There were two important omissions from the signatories – G.

T. Knight and H. Kingscote. Knight, described by a contemporary rhymster:

> As a bowler first-rate, as a bat far from vile,
> And he bowls in the new march of intellect style.

was a Kentish cricketer, who was repeatedly no-balled for bowling round-arm. He wrote several letters to the *Sporting Magazine* in 1827 defending round-arm bowling by explaining that batsman had completely mastered the old under-arm bowlers and run-getting was steadily increasing; matches in some cases were now lasting five days and the remedy in the past to the domination of the bat was to increase the size of the wicket, but there must be a limit to this adjustment. Knight played for England in the match against Sussex at Lord's and was the most successful England bowler, though the County won by three wickets. Kingscote, the other cricketer who did not sign the declaration, was the President of MCC in 1827 and one of the promoters of the matches against Sussex. He lead the progressive wing of the premier Club against the diehards led by William Ward. Kingscote persuaded the players who had signed the declaration to recant and the third meeting between Sussex and England took place at Brighton. This time, with Knight's bowling proving again successful, England won and their batsmen mastered Lillywhite and Broadbridge. Denison, another diehard wrote:

> [England's] second hands, however, did the hearts good of all the Old School, convincing them that this mode of delivering the ball only wanted once to be shaken off to lose the power of its effect. Saunders, Budd and Beagley beat it away, and made a capital example of it.

Later in 1827 Sussex played Kent at Sevenoaks, with Knight appearing for Kent and Lillywhite and Broadbridge for Sussex, all three bowling round-arm. Denison felt that true cricket was dead: 'This noble triumvirate, like their revolutionary chums, have destroyed all hopes of ever seeing good taste adorn cricket society again.' Though differently phrased, this is a theme which has continued throughout the history of the game until the present time.

In May 1828 G. T. Knight put the proposition before the MCC that Rule 10 be changed to:

> That the ball shall be bowled. If it be thrown or jerked, or if any part of the hand or arm be above the shoulder at the time of delivery, the umpire shall call 'no ball'.

This removed the word 'underarm' and the phrase 'and any part of the back of the hand uppermost' from the old Rule as well as changing 'elbow' to 'shoulder'.

At the specially convened meeting on 9 May 1828, the proposal by Knight was hotly debated and ended in a compromise. The Meeting agreed to delete the word 'underarm' from the Law and also the phrase 'and any part of the back of the hand uppermost' but refused to change 'elbow' to 'shoulder', so that the new Law still insisted that the hand should not be above the elbow when the ball was delivered.

This compromise achieved nothing. It still meant that the bowling of Lillywhite and Broadbridge was illegal and few if any of the younger players paid the slightest attention to the MCC ruling. In 1832 Alfred Mynn played his first match at Lord's and within a year or two he became the most effective bowler in England, bowling with his arm parallel with his shoulder. Even to the diehards the Law preventing bowlers raising their hand above their elbow was now totally ridiculous.

The issue was finally forced when some bowlers began to deliver the ball overarm. William Denison noted:

> So long as this practice was confined to so accomplished a bowler as Lillywhite, and the best of the Mary-le-bone players, there was little, if any harm done, beyond this, that it was a violation of a rule, which ought not to have been permitted even in their persons. As the old saying runs, 'If you have a rule, keep to it, stick to it.' The infringement, being tolerated at 'Lord's,' soon obtained with other bowlers, and after Mr. Mynn's debut when every bowler thought that pace not steadiness, was the acmé of perfection, what with the endeavour to bowl as fast as that gentleman, and the delivery being mostly above the shoulder, the bowling arrived at such a pitch of violence, recklessness, and danger, that the

committee of the Mary-le-bone Club felt it to be necessary to impose a restrictive law against the elevation of the hand in the delivery.

The new Law read:

> The ball must be bowled. If it be thrown or jerked, or if the hand be above the shoulder in the delivery, the umpire must call 'No ball'.

That Law was passed on 14 May 1835. Still the bowlers had little regard for the Law and several of the leaders were now bowling with the arm above the shoulder. Ten more years went by. The MCC made yet another attempt to keep the bowlers in check. On 9 June 1845 the following Law was passed:

> The ball must be bowled, not thrown or jerked, and the hand must not be above the shoulder in delivery; and whenever the bowler shall so closely infringe on this rule in either of the above particulars, as to make it difficult for the umpire at the bowler's wicket to judge whether the ball has been delivered within the true intent and meaning of this rule or not, the umpire shall call 'No Ball'.

There seems to have been a temporary check on bowlers delivering the ball above shoulder height after this latest revision was introduced. Haygarth noted after a match between MCC and Western Counties at Lord's in June 1846, in which 16 no balls were recorded:

> Many no balls occurred in the matches at *Lord's* about this time, the Umpires having strict orders to call all bowlers who were too high. The infringement of law 10 was, however, soon winked at and it became a dead letter . . .

In the above note Haygarth puts 'Lord's' in italics, to emphasise the fact that away from headquarters, few umpires even then enforced this new amendment.

In 1863, the MCC made a final attempt to turn back the clocks:

> I. That the MCC umpires be directed to watch the bowling strictly in all matches on Lord's Ground and in all MCC

matches elsewhere with a view to carry out the provisions of Law X with impartiality, and to the best of their judgment.

II. That in forming their judgment as to the fairness of any bowler, they shall attend particularly to the height of his hand as it passes his body in the last swing of the arm before delivery.

III. That the Committee will receive complaints which may be made to them respecting any alleged erroneous or improper decisions of umpires employed by the MCC, and will deal with proved cases of incapacity or unfairness; but the committee will decline to give an opinion as to the fairness or unfairness of any particular bowler, as they believe that interference with the independence of umpires would be injurious to cricket.

IV. That these resolutions be printed, and a copy given to each of the MCC players.

This confusion over the height of the bowling arm, which had now lasted about forty years, provoked the notion that a 'Cricket Parliament' should be set up. This parliament should take over the task of revising the Laws of the game from the MCC. There was a long debate in the correspondence columns of *The Sporting Life* during the winter of 1863–64 and a meeting was held at the London Tavern on 2 June 1864, but the whole idea fizzled out.

The major bowler affected by the retention of the Law forbidding the bowler's hand to be above the shoulder was Ted Willsher of Kent and as has been noted in the first Chapter of this book, he was no-balled for throwing during the Surrey v England match at the Oval in 1862 by John Lillywhite, the England team refusing to continue the game until another umpire was appointed in Lillywhite's place. In the following year, when Willsher played at Lord's in the England v United All England match, the crowd was inflated by those who came purely to see if Willsher would be no-balled. He wasn't and Caffyn noted: 'it soon became evident to the spectators that there would be no sensation and I believe many of them were disappointed accordingly.'

Willsher felt however, that he was victimised for much of his career; the famous umpire, Robert Thoms, stated:

> There is very little doubt that his bowling would not at all times stand the scrutiny of a 'Binocular' in the then existing law, which enacted that the hand should not be above the shoulder. Willsher often pathetically remarked that he had been born too soon: and, perhaps, to a certain extent he had cause to think so, for he lived to see chuckers, half-chuckers, windmills and pounding down bowlers, have a good time of it, whilst he, a bowler with a strictly fair delivery, as regards bowling had to be settled for occasionally delivering the ball above the shoulder. This to me is not a pleasant theme to dwell upon, and so I will at once run it short with a full stop.

Thoms wrote these words in an obituary to Willsher in October 1885, when yet another row over the fairness of bowlers' deliveries was raging. On 10 June 1864, yet another meeting of MCC members finally conceded that bowlers could raise the delivery arm above the shoulders:

> At the conclusion of the above match, on the afternoon of Friday 10 June, an influential meeting of the members of the Marylebone Club was held in the Tennis Court to legislate on the proposed motion of Mr Charles Marsham to repeal the old rule and substitute another, abolishing all restriction as to height of hand in delivery. Earl Dudley (late Lord Ward), President, presided. The subject was duly and ably debated, the old law was repealed, and on a division (27 against 20) it was decided that Rule X of the Laws of Cricket should henceforth stand as follows:
> 'The balls must be bowled; if thrown or jerked, the Umpire shall call "No ball".'

The following was published in some of the sporting papers:

> LAW X.
> On June 10th 1864, according to announcement, a very important meeting, of considerable interest to cricketers in general, was held in the Tennis-court adjoining Lord's Ground, to take into consideration the above law.

Lord Dudley presided, and having stated the object of the meeting, Mr. Charles Marsham rose, and read some correspondence from various clubs, expressing their opinion on Law X. He then gave his own views on the subject, and concluded by moving that the law as it stood should be rescinded, and that the following be substituted:–

'The ball must be bowled; if thrown or jerked, the umpire must call "No ball".'

Mr. H. Perkins briefly seconded the motion.

Mr. FitzGerald (Hon Sec of MCC) said he was opposed to high bowling, and there ought to be restrictions upon it. He attributed all the large scores that were now made to high bowling, and thought that there were not so many good bowlers as there used to be, and that high bowling was much inferior to low. He opposed the motion. Mr. R. P. Broughton after some preliminary remarks, moved an amendment which was tantamount to the law remaining as it stood, which is as follows:

'The ball must be bowled; if thrown or jerked, or if the bowler in the actual delivery of the ball, or in the action immediately preceding the delivery, shall raise his hand or arm above his shoulder, the umpire shall call "No ball".'

Mr. R. Kynaston seconded the amendment.

The Hon. F. Ponsonby said that this was not a new question. He could recollect that thirty years ago bowling was as high then as now, and although they tried to keep the arm down, the umpires failed to enforce the law. Umpires were frequently abused for not doing their duty, and as there was a diversity of opinion among many persons as to the fairness or unfairness of a bowler, it was not to be supposed that the umpire could decide so as to give satisfaction at all. To allow high bowling, it was said by some, would be dangerous on rough ground; but care should be taken that grounds should not be rough. He strongly supported the motion. The Hon. R. Grimston made some very appropriate remarks in favour of the motion, and said it was true, as Mr. Ponsonby stated, they legislated for themselves (the MCC), and he had no doubt the high position in which the club stood would be upheld by other clubs in carrying out the laws.

The Hon. F. Cavendish said he thought Mr. Marsham and Mr. Ponsonby had fully explained what was practicable, and it was no use trying to enforce what they could not carry out. He should give his support to the motion.

A Member supported the amendment of Mr. Broughton, and thought that one more effort might be made to carry the laws into effect as they stood. Cries of 'Divide, divide!'.

The Chairman rose, and most ably commented upon the question, inclining much to the opinion of Mr. Broughton.

His Lordship was about to put the amendment to the vote, when Mr. Broughton withdrew it.

The Chairman then put the motion, which was carried by a majority of 27 to 20, amid much cheering.

Law XXIV, relative to 'leg b.w.,' was to have been discussed, but the motion was withdrawn.

It will be noted however that even now the majority for the motion was only 27 to 20.

The problem as to the height of the bowler's arm had finally been settled, but it was sadly not too long before the argument about unfair bowling transferred itself to the phrase 'if thrown or jerked'. On the whole, the MCC had made a terrible mess of the troubles connected to the height of the bowling arm. Rait Kerr in his book *The Laws of Cricket* wrote:

It may be possible to justify the MCC's policy in regard to round-arm bowling in the period 1810 to 1835, but it is very difficult to believe that the situation which developed later could not have been better handled – as a result the years 1840 to 1864 probably represent the very worst period of MCC control of the game, and might well have proved disastrous to cricket.

When in about 1880, the problem of bowlers 'throwing' the ball by means of bending and straightening their arm to add extra speed to the delivery was beginning to occur in County cricket, the MCC were very loath to act in the matter, mindful of their previous muddled deliberations and more especially of the fact that many umpires had ignored the various alterations in the Laws, even at Lord's itself.

The magazine *Cricket*, which was founded in 1882, was one of the leading voices which advocated the removal of bowlers with 'doubtful deliveries' from the County scene. The Surrey v Lancashire match at the Oval in August 1882 produced the following comments:

The very strong expression of opinion at the Oval on Monday shows really how necessary it is that the questionable style of delivery now generally practised, chiefly from the impunity the throwing order of bowlers enjoys, should be really and firmly taken in hand. I am not defending the ebullition effecting Crossland's action produced on the Surrey ground, but at the same time it may do good if it helps to force on the authorities the urgency of satisfying the public mind with regard to the very obvious and frequent infringement of the laws defining bowling. Differences of opinion exist among the best judges as to whether certain bowlers have a fair delivery or not, and it is not my intention to argue whether certain men, known in the slang of the cricket field as 'chuckers', throw or not. My contention is only that there are many players, amateurs as well as professional, who are notoriously under suspicion, and in the interests of the public, and for the general satisfaction, it is well worthy of the consideration of the Marylebone Club whether some definite action should not be taken to prove the fairness or unfairness of that class of bowlers of which Crossland is the type. It is really useless to urge that the umpires are the proper judges. In the first place, there are few of them competent to decide such a point; in the second, the man who would have the courage of his opinions to no-ball anyone, in my opinion has not existed since John Lillywhite.

The comments caused strong counter-criticism:

I have, unhappily for my peace of mind, by my remarks last week anent Crossland, brought down a very hornet's nest about my ears. Letters, irate as well as expostulatory, have reached me from Lancashire cricketers and supporters of cricket in the county. 'Why is it thus?' to use one of Artemus Ward's quaint phrases, 'Whence this thusness?' I have been audacious enough to hint that Crossland's delivery is open to suspicion. One correspondent accuses me of bias because I have not named Messrs. Tuke and Evans in the same category. I was particular to say that I only regarded Crossland as the type of a fast increasing school, quite as popular in the South as in the North. I am reasonable I think, in assuming that Crossland would have played for England had his bowling been considered quite fair. I have no bias in the matter, and I say distinctly that there are several cricketers in the South whose delivery is quite as questionable as Crossland's. I hope that this positive assertion will allay the anger I have caused. If not I shall try to carry out into effect Longfellow's precept of 'Knowing how sublime a thing it is to suffer and be strong'.

A sudden injury to Morley, the England fast bowler, just prior to the picking of the England team to play Australia at the Oval in the only Test of 1882 commencing 28 August, gave the selectors food for thought. The obvious choice to take Morley's place was Crossland – in terms of figures he was the outstanding bowler of 1882 with 112 wickets, av. 10.06 – but the Australian captain, Murdoch, had already spoken out about the number of bowlers in England who 'threw' the ball and said that they certainly would not be allowed on Australian grounds. The English selectors took the hint and ignored Crossland. This, the magazine *Cricket* stated in an Editorial, 'may fairly be considered a proof that they [the selectors] did not consider his style strictly within the letter of the law.'

Lord Harris was as outspoken as *Cricket* on the subject. In 1883 the MCC instructed a sub-committee to revise the Laws 'by defining terms, supplying omissions, and better wording, but without altering the spirit of the game.' The sub-committee drew up a revised draft and this was circulated to all County Clubs, as well as authorities in Australia and the United States. Although Lord Harris was on the sub-committee, he was not satisfied with the draft proposals for Law X and wrote to the magazine *Cricket* in May 1883:

Sir, – I shall be obliged if you will give me the opportunity of making public my intention, at the general meeting of the

MCC which must be summoned to considered the laws of cricket as amended by a committee of that club, of moving to amend Law X by the addition of the words to this effect, 'If in the opinion of the umpire there is any doubt as to the fairness of the delivery he shall call 'no-ball'.

Faithfully yours,
Harris.

The magazine *The Field* was worried that if Lord Harris's amendment was passed, then umpires would be divided into two factions – those who thought Crossland, Evans, Mycroft etc, threw, and those of a contrary opinion. This division of umpires would cause more problems.

The MCC instructed umpires to enforce Law 10 strictly but this instruction had little effect – the Editor of *Cricket* pointed out a fortnight after the instructions had been issued that no bowler in first-class cricket had been no-balled for throwing, though a Kent Colt in a trial had been no-balled by Robert Thoms, only to change ends and bowl without hindrance.

To add to the confusion, Nottinghamshire County Cricket Club had objected to Crossland playing for Lancashire, not on the grounds of his bowling action, but because as a native of Nottinghamshire and also a resident of the county, save in the cricket season, he was not qualified to represent Lancashire. The MCC ruled that Crossland was properly qualified, but that Nottinghamshire were justified in raising the matter.

The season of 1883 drew to its close without any headway being made. A meeting of County representatives was held at Lord's on 11 December. Lord Harris was in the chair. Two resolutions were put after a long discussion. The first was that 'the undermentioned counties agree among themselves not to employ any bowler whose action is at all doubtful'. Six counties voted for, whilst Lancashire, Gloucestershire and Sussex abstained. The other resolution that 'the matter of unfair bowling be left to the MCC' was defeated by 5 to 4. The defeat was due to the fact that MCC would be over-ruling the umpires, which was not regarded as desirable. The meeting had some effect. *Lillywhite's Cricketers' Companion*, reporting on the 1884 season noted:

We are glad to be able to say that there was a decided abatement of the throwing scandal, and it certainly seems that the resolution to which the representatives of Yorkshire, Kent, Derby, Middlesex, Nottinghamshire and Surrey subscribed, in the December of 1883, has borne good fruit. Of course there were occasional instances of unfair bowling to be met with, but that there was an improvement no one who carefully watched the season's cricket can deny. Crossland, the player whose style had excited the most discussion, still bowled in a way which was open to the gravest objection. Some little excitement was created during the season by the fact of his being 'no-balled' in a local match at Sutton-in-Ashfield, his native place. No umpire, however, in first-class matches had the courage to interfere with him. If the Counties be really in earnest, there is no reason why throwing in England should not be absolutely got rid of. We sincerely trust that there will be no going back on this important question, for the permission of throwing could not but have a most disastrous effect upon the well-being of the game. The thanks of all true cricketers are due to Lord Harris for his energetic and persevering action in this matter.

Lord Harris did not rest on his laurels. After Kent had played Lancashire at Old Trafford in May 1885, his Lordship, Captain of Kent, sent a letter to the Lancashire County Cricket Club stating that he was of the opinion that Crossland and Nash, the two leading Lancashire bowlers, bowled unfairly during the match and that the return game due to be played in August was therefore cancelled. Furthermore Kent would not again play Lancashire 'until a more satisfactory state of things maintains.'

Lord Harris had now taken matters into his own hands, both the MCC and the umpires being unable or unwilling to solve the problem. Nottinghamshire had refused to make any fixtures with Lancashire in 1884 due to the row over Crossland's qualifications and Middlesex also declined to play Lancashire – that county was therefore becoming increasingly isolated.

An exchange of cards over the Christmas of 1883 between Notts and Lancashire did nothing to improve relationships. Lancashire's read:

CRICKET RULES Drawn up by the Notts County Cricket Club 1883–4.

Rule 1: That in playing Lancashire the Lancashire men shall not be allowed to use bats but only broom handles.

Rule 2: That Lancashire shall not be allowed any bowlers, and if so no stumps be used; and the Notts captain to select the bowler.

Rule 3: That both umpires shall be strictly Notts men.

Rule 4: That in case there is any fear that Notts should lose, even under these rules, the Notts men do leave the field and refuse to finish the game.

It was a somewhat daring procedure on Lancashire's part to send such a greeting for retort was easy, and was made as follows, which was sent to Manchester as a New Year's card:

LANCASHIRE COUNTY CRICKET

The only rules necessary for players in the County Eleven are that they shall neither have been born in, nor reside in, Lancashire. Sutton-in-Ashfield men will have the preference.

Nottinghamshire again objected to Crossland playing for Lancashire on the grounds that he did not reside in that County. The MCC heard evidence from local rate and rent collectors, the village policeman and the local squire and this time decided that Crossland did not reside continuously and regularly in Lancashire and was therefore not qualified for that County. This ruling was made in the middle of the 1885 season and Lancashire immediately dropped Crossland from their team – the county also dropped Nash, their other controversial bowler, in the same year. In 1886 Nottinghamshire resumed matches with Lancashire.

The crisis died down, but once more there was only a lull. *Wisden's Almanack* covering the 1894 season contained a long article, entitled 'Throwing in First-Class Cricket'. The opening paragraph explains the situation:

In conversation with several first-class cricketers during the past season I heard such serious complaints as to the unfairness of certain bowlers that I thought it advisable, on the principle that has several times before this been followed in Wisden's Almanack when a question has been ripe for discussion, to write to a number of the best-known amateurs, asking them for an opinion on the subject. . . . It was not argued by any of the cricketers I met in the summer that the evil had assumed anything like the same proportions as when Lord Harris, some years ago, took such strong action in the matter, but there seemed a strong feeling that the mischief was certainly cropping up again, and that, as a prudent medical officer endeavours to grapple with an outbreak of disease while it is still confined to a small area, it was well that something should be done before things became worse than they were in 1894. Lest it should be thought that I am dealing merely with generalities, and, as it were, fighting the air, I may state that the bowlers of whom I heard the most serious complaints were Mold, Captain Hedley, Mr C. B. Fry and Hardstaff. In dealing with a question so delicate, I did not write to any professional players, feeling that it would be placing them in a very false position to ask them to express an opinion.

When the Australians came to England in 1896, it was quite obvious that the disease had spread to their bowlers:

Up to last season one of the special virtues of Australian bowling was its unimpeachable fairness. Despite the evil example set by many English throwers team after team came over to England without a bowler to whose delivery exception could be taken, but unhappily things are no longer as they once were. We have not the least hesitation in saying that a fast bowler with the action of Jones, or a slow bowler with a delivery so open to question as McKibbin, would have found no place in the earlier elevens that came to England. Jones's bowling is, to our mind, radically unfair, as we cannot conceive a ball being fairly bowled at a pace of an express train with a bent arm. The faults of our own bowlers with regard to throwing have been so many and grievous that we are extremely glad Jones was allowed to go through the season unchallenged, but now that the tour is a thing of the past, it is only a duty to speak plainly on the matter.

The Australians were, in comparison with MCC, quick to act. Spofforth, the greatest Australian fast bowler of his day, wrote a letter to *The Sporting Life* condemning McKibbin's action in the most uncompromising terms and James Phillips, the noted Australian umpire, no-balled Jones for throwing in October 1897. As if encouraged by the Australian efforts to stamp out throwing, the English umpires in 1898 no-balled C. B. Fry in three separate matches and Hopkins of Warwickshire was also no-balled.

In the two following years umpires continued to no-ball various first-class county cricketers, but the evil was only ended as a result of a meeting of County captains on 10 December 1900, when the captains agreed among themselves not to use certain bowlers and drew up a list. In 1901 only one bowler was no-balled – Mold of Lancashire. The following December the MCC issued a circular as follows:

ILLEGAL BOWLING: The MCC Committee have given further careful consideration to the question of illegal bowling, and are of the opinion that the decision of the Captains in 1900 has done so much good in discouraging this practice that it is unnecessary to suggest any drastic measure at present.

They hope that the County Cricket Executives will, in future, decline to play bowlers with doubtful deliveries, and thus remove the probability of any further infringement of Law 48. Should an occasion arise when an Umpire by no-balling a bowler makes it clear that he is protesting against his deliveries, they think the only course open to the Captain is to take such bowler off, otherwise the proper spirit of the game cannot be preserved. To meet the contingency of any flagrant case of illegal bowling arising in the future, the following proposal has been made, and the Counties are invited to express an opinion thereon. 'The Counties shall authorize their Captains to deal with the question and, if at any meeting convened, with notice that it will be brought up, the Captains shall decide by a majority of 2 to 1 that any bowler has been guilty of illegal bowling, they shall 'name' him and recommend his suspension for at least a season, and refer it to the MCC Committee for confirmation'

Yours faithfully

F. E. Lacey, Sec, MCC

The problem of 'throwing' was then effectively ended for a period of nearly fifty years.

4 The Great Australian Row

To the independent, freebooting clique that made up the Australian teams of the 1880s and 1890s, the very thought of a 'Board of Control' was an anathema. For 25 years the cricketers had selected their own teams to tour England, taken the risks, and enjoyed the substantial profits that accrued. The do-gooders cast an eye on all the money which was disappearing into the players' pockets and in some cases straight from there to the local bar. 'The profits from the tours should be ploughed back into the game and help in its developments,' they cried. Certain players, who felt that they deserved to play for Australia, but were ignored by the clique yelled, 'Foul! A team can't truly claim to represent Australia and yet not be chosen by authorised selection process.' So the disgruntled, cold-shouldered, players joined with the do-gooders and the eventual outcome was a Board of Control diametrically opposed to the leading Australian Test cricketers of the day. A classic setting for an explosive confrontation – and so it was to prove.

The 'administration' of cricket in Australia began about 1857 with the founding by William Tunks and Harry Hilliard in Sydney of the New South Wales Cricket Association. The main object of the Association was threefold: to arrange the inter-colonial fixtures against Victoria, to select the New South Wales side and to prepare a suitable home venue. Victoria did not have such an Association and when, in 1863, an umpiring dispute during the inter-colonial match at Sydney resulted in two of the Victorian players walking off in the middle of the game, the New South Wales Cricket Association, who were keen to settle the argument, found it impossible to discuss the matter with Victoria. The result was that the aggrieved players could not be reconciled and plans to arrange the next years' fixture had to be abandoned.

In October 1864, R. W. Wardill of Melbourne set up a Victorian Cricketers' Association and opened negotiations to resume the match with New South Wales. Although the original Victorian Association soon collapsed this object was achieved. From the Association and its successors eventually grew the present Victorian Cricket Association. South Australia set up an Association in 1871 and the remaining colonies followed suit over the next twenty years, with Tasmania being divided between North and South.

Of the three senior Associations, only the South Australian one was completely master of its own kingdom, being the leaseholder of the Adelaide Oval, promoter of other sports as well as cricket, and financially sound. The New South Wales Association had to compete with the Trustees of Sydney Cricket Ground, the Association being tenants, on somewhat unfavourable terms, of the Trustees. In Melbourne the position was even more tangled. The Melbourne Cricket Club was strong, and the Victorian Cricket Association, which was financially very insecure, had little control over the Club – at one stage it was proposed that the VCA disband and hand over whatever authority it had to the Melbourne Club.

The relative strengths of the Victorian Cricket Association against the Melbourne Club and the New South Wales Cricket Association against the Sydney Trustees can be judged by the fact that arrangements for the English team touring Australia in the 1880s were made by the Club or the Trustees and not by the Associations – an English side being invited out almost every other season. In 1887/8 the two sponsors clashed, both inviting the English touring team and both refusing to bow to the other. Both touring teams lost vast sums of money. The Melbourne Club, as the most powerful cricket organisation in Australia, also provided the backing for several Australian teams to tour England and sent teams also to New Zealand.

When Lord Sheffield took his English team out to Australia in 1891–92 – the first such side since the disaster of 1887–88 – the Australians set up the Australian Cricket Council, which helped to organise the Sheffield Shield Competition. The

Council was however little more than a talking shop, taking few administrative decisions and merely agreeing with various arrangements already arrived at by the powers in Sydney and Melbourne.

In 1898–99, the English authorities set up a national 'Test Selection' committee to pick teams for home Internationals (previously, selection had rested with each ground authority) and in 1903, the MCC took over the selection and administration of the major English overseas touring teams. Inspired to some extent by this example, the Victorian Cricket Association proposed a conference of the three major Associations to discuss the idea. The Conference was held on 2 January 1905. It was agreed to set up a Board of Control and also, on a proposal from South Australia, that the financial obligations of the Board should be limited and that the players should be represented on the Board. After the Conference, however, the New South Wales Cricket Association and the Victorian Cricket Association objected to these two proposals by the South Australians. Therefore when the delegates met for the first Meeting of the new Board, the South Australians refused to come, stating that the whole project was invalid because of their absence. South Australia was ignored and the New South Wales Cricket Association and the Victorian Cricket Association invited the Queensland Association to join the Board.

Between the Conference in January and the first meeting of the new Board in May, the Australian team to tour England in the summer of 1905 needed to be selected and organised. The Associations offered to advance money for the visit, but the players at a meeting decided not to accept this offer, borrowing money instead from the Melbourne Cricket Club. Frank Laver, the Victorian cricketer, was appointed by the team as player-manager. The opinions of the various Associations were not asked for, and New South Wales in particular felt slighted.

The players, having arranged the 1905 tour with the aid of the Melbourne Club and having organised a dozen previous visits themselves, thought that the creation of a Board of Control was utterly unnecessary, as did the Melbourne Club itself. During the early part of 1905 it was in one of its perennial conflicts with the Victorian Cricket Association. The Victorian

Cricket Association, realising that the new Board would be a mere rubber stamp without the powerful Melbourne Club, put the following proposals to the Club:

1. All Inter-state and international matches would be played on Melbourne Cricket Ground.
2. The Club would receive reasonable financial reward for the use of the Ground for international matches.
3. The Melbourne Club would have a seat on the Board.

The Australasian published the following report in April, 1906:

The last phase of cricket in Australia, but especially in Victoria, is always worse than the stage immediately preceding it. The negotiations for the formation of a Board of Control were understood to have been settled some time ago – but the settlement was something in the nature of an armistice in battle, which merely enables the combatants to collect their energies and begin afresh. Incidentally, the armistice enables the fighters also to collect their dead, and if this battle continues there will be need for the same solemn office in connection with the remains of cricket. All that is left of a once live game will be fit for little else than to carry off to a mortuary for decent interment. The game must have had wonderful vitality to begin with, or it never could have stood the buffeting its misguided friends are giving it. Finality with the Board of Control seems as far off as ever, if one may judge from the tone of the last meeting of the Cricket Association. 'Come outside!' appeared to be the main argument, and though that resource seems to be a little out of date in a deliberating body, it has sometimes the merit of being conclusive. The inside work – if one may so class the innumerable conferences and conversations on the subject – has produced nothing but a heated atmosphere.

Reading the various press comments and views put forward on the subject produces nothing but confusion. The magazine *Cricket* in May 1906 sums up the feeling:

It is simply impossible to say what is the latest development of the situation in Australia, for the cablegrams, press and private, differ to a degree which is unusual. Hence it is stated that several players have been suspended, disqualified, excommunicated by the New South Wales Cricketers' Association; that no players have been suspended etc; that time has been given to the recalcitrant players to repent of their misdeeds; that the Melbourne Cricket Club has sent an invitation to the Marylebone Cricket Club to send out a team this autumn, and that the offer has been declined; that no such invitation was ever sent; that a rival Board of Control has been formed by clubs which would not join the original Board; that no rival Board has been formed; that the players who accepted the offer of the Melbourne Club, and were suspended, have gone down on their knees to apologise, and have thrown over the Melbourne Club.

The only things which seem incontrovertible in connection with the Board are that the original Board consists of New South Wales (2 representatives), Victoria Cricket Association (2 representatives) and Queensland (1 representative); that the Melbourne Club was to have joined the Board, but jilted when ordered to elect its representatives; that South Australia and Tasmania have declined to join the Board. All other information seems indefinite and not to be relied on.

Various bodies in Australia were keen that the MCC send a team to Australia in the season of 1906/7, but the conflict between these various bodies was such that a stalemate continued through May and June of 1906. At the beginning of July however, the Melbourne Club and the Victorian Cricket Association agreed to support the Board's invitation to Lord's to send an English team, provided the New South Wales Cricket Association remove the suspensions they had placed on several players.

The Australian Board finally sorted out its internal differences and on 21 August sent a cable to Lord's inviting the English team to Australia. The English reply was that it was much too late to organise such a tour, but that a tour might be possible in 1907–08.

The *Melbourne Herald* suggested that England were deliberately withholding from making a tour to 'punish Australian cricketers', which at least to Engish minds appeared to be a very obscure view of the whole affair. The Prime Minister of New South Wales made a last-minute appeal to the Marylebone Club at the beginning of September, but the position remained unaltered.

In October New South Wales Cricket Club adopted a set of new rules designed to keep a stronger control over the activities of players. The rules included one which forbade any member of the Association arranging matches with any teams outside New South Wales without the sanction of the Association and permission would not be granted if the match was not approved by the State Association in which it was proposed to play the match.

The proposed English visit took place in 1907–08. The Australian Board had now put its own house in order. The driving force behind the Board was W. P. McElhone, the Board's Secretary. Rowland Bowen, the historian, describes McElhone: 'as tenacious as a terrier after a rat, and as slippery as an eel or as evasive as a bird in controversy.' The Board appointed a selection Committee of three to choose Australia's teams for the 1907–08 series – Joe Darling of South Australia, Frank Iredale of New South Wales and Peter McAlister of Victoria. Darling had captained Australia in England in 1905 and was in his final season in first-class cricket; Iredale, a former Test player, had been retired from first-class matches for several years, McAlister, who had played twice for Australia in the 1903–04 series, was still playing for Victoria and was bitter about being left out of Darling's 1905 team to England. At the same meeting the Board rejected an application from the players for representation on the Board, a rejection which did nothing to improve the Board's image with the players, who still thought its existence unnecessary.

McAlister managed to select himself for four of the five Tests of the 1907–08 series, though his scores – 10 and 15; 28 and 17; 37 and 4; 3 and 41 – placed him 12th in the Test batting averages, considerably below any of the other established batsmen. Since he was in his 39th year, it would have seemed more sensible to try a younger man after he had failed once or twice.

When the time came to select the team for the 1909 Australian tour to England, the Board decided on the selection committee of McAlister, Iredale and Clem Hill. The press could not understand the reasoning behind this trio. Both Monty Noble and Victor Trumper, two of Australia's most famous players, offered themselves as candidates, but were rejected in favour of McAlister, whose knowledge of cricket in England was negligible.

Before the selectors could proceed with their work, several of the leading Australian players objected to the proposed financial arrangements. For some time it looked as if the tour would have to be abandoned, but wiser councils prevailed and eventually a team was chosen, with McAlister as both a playing member and treasurer. The players, as in 1905, picked Frank Laver as their manager. This right for the players to choose a manager was one of the original rules laid down when the Board was established.

Laver and McAlister, who both came from the East Melbourne Club, had been great friends, but their friendship had become soured in 1905, when McAlister had been passed over for the tour to England. He believed that Laver had been behind his non-selection. To have the two officials of the 1909 touring side at loggerheads looked ominous and so it was to prove.

McAlister also got himself appointed vice-captain over the heads of Trumper and Armstrong, which caused ill-feeling amongst the team as a whole. The results of the tour showed McAlister up for what he was – a cricketer past his best. He had a very moderate tour with a highest score of only 85 and played in two Tests. Laver played brilliantly and topped the bowling averages with 70 wickets, average 14.97.

Although Laver was the player's manager, the whole of the financial affairs of the tour should have been looked after by McAlister on behalf of the Board. For some unknown reasons however, McAlister kept no accurate account books, so that when the team returned to Australia and the Board asked McAlister for some financial details, he was unable to supply them. McAlister claimed that Laver had kept an account book, but refused to allow him to see it, on the grounds that it contained only private business of personal concern to the players. Laver contradicted this in so far as he stated that McAlister was shown the account books. This fact was confirmed by the team's captain, Noble. The Board then wrote to Laver asking to borrow his account books, and Laver, whilst not refusing, said that they contained private transactions. The Secretary of the Board replied that he would therefore not insist on seeing the books. That appeared to be the end of the matter.

At the end of 1911, the whole business was aired again, when it was alleged that Laver refused to let the Board look at the account books, though, through Clem Hill, Laver actually let the Board have the books.

England were touring Australia during 1911–12, and in the following summer of 1912 both Australia and South Africa were due to come to England for the Triangular Tournament between the three countries. The Board appointed Hill, McAlister and Iredale as selectors for the 1912 tour to England, nominated Hill and Trumper as captain and vice-captain of the tourists, then stated that the players would not need a Manager, the Board selecting a secretary who would also take on that role.

In the wake of these announcements, Hill, McAlister and Iredale met to choose the Australian side for the Fourth Test of the 1911–12 series to be played at Melbourne commencing 9 February. In the middle of the meeting McAlister told Hill that he was the worst captain Australia had ever had. Hill stood up, punching McAlister in the face as he did so. McAlister retaliated, and the pair were in a clinch perilously near the window when Smith, who was taking the minutes, saw the danger of them falling out into the street thirty feet below. Smith grabbed Hill. Iredale, who had found himself pinned to the wall by the table, extricated himself and pulled McAlister away. Hill shook himself loose and marched out of the room, saying that he resigned forthwith and leaving McAlister to nurse his bruised face.

The selectorial trio had been at loggerheads when they met to pick the team for the previous Test. Hill wanted to include Matthews and Macartney, whilst McAlister wanted Roy Minnett to play. McAlister ended by sending the following wire to Hill:

My team as forwarded yesterday. Still opposed to Macartney's inclusion. If Iredale [the third selector] agrees with you as to Macartney's inclusion, I favour yourself standing down, not Minnett.

To send such a telegram to the captain of the Australian side suggesting he should drop out of the team, because the selectors were unable to decide on who should fill the eleventh place, would seem total stupidity even if the captain was not a major player in the team; in this case Clem Hill was one of best batsmen in Australia and had made 46 and 65 in the First Test of the Series, taking Australia to a 146-run victory.

Iredale solved this impasse by suggesting that Minnett played and Macartney stood down. However, Clem Hill, or his associates, published the offending telegram and this brought the divisions between the selectors right into the open. The magazine *Cricket*, published in England on 27 January 1912 noted:

It was asking too much of human nature to expect Messrs Hill and McAlister to work in harmony together . . . As selectors of the last Australian team for England (1909), they differed very strongly on a matter that it was impossible to keep outside the range of personalities – to wit, McAlister's claim to a place in the side. Such things are not easily forgotten.

The Board wrote to certain leading players to ask if they would go on the tour – Hill, Trumper, Armstrong, Cotter, Carter and Ransford then said that they would not decide until the Board confirmed or denied that the players could take their own Manager as in 1909, in other words Frank Laver. The Board, in something of a quandary, said nothing.

On 30 March 1912 *Cricket* gives the latest news:

At half-past the eleventh hour it was announced from Sydney that after all Victor Trumper and Vernon Ransford might possibly join the Australian team for England. But within twenty-four hours came an explicit contradiction from Ransford, who stated that he would not make the trip unless invitations were again extended not only to Trumper, but to Hill, Armstrong, Carter and Cotter.

This was naturally out of the question. However anxious we may all have been to see the crack Australian players again – and I don't think that their welcome here would have been any the less hearty for their squabble with the Board – we must all admit that the Board would have stultified itself in the opinion of three continents if it had done as Ransford suggested. He and Trumper might have been added to the team. The whole six could not have been, by any possibility. To have forced any of the men chosen in their places to stand down for them at the last moment would have been the grossest injustice.

The whole affair is a tragic pity. Both sides are as far in the wrong as it is well possible for both sides in any quarrel to be. The Board have had over two years in which to clear up the matter of Frank Laver's alleged insubordination, and to leave the clearing it up till the time for choosing the team came was simply asking for trouble. Then, too, they went outside their legal powers as it would seem, in appointing a representative who was also to be manager, which barred the players from choosing a manager for themselves. But this, as may be easily understood, was because the Board would not have Laver at any price.

On the other side, the players – the recalcitrant six, as Iredale styled them – stuck to Laver with something very like fanatic loyalty. They argued that he was indispensable to the team, which on the face of it was slightly absurd; they saw that, with a majority for the Board on the Selection Committee, he had no chance of being chosen as a player; and they believed that by holding together they could force the Board to accept him as player-manager. They were mistaken, however.

Most of us hold that there should be a Board of Cricket Control in Australia. But few like entirely the methods of the Board, as now constituted. A man who has been for years a popular idol is apt to be a trifle self-willed. But it is a fair question whether jumping on him with both feet is likely to convert him to sweet reasonableness. The 'rebels' felt that, having backed Laver in his tacit defiance of the Board, they could not desert him. One fancies that a word from Laver might have put that right. One is almost certain that a less arbitrary attitude on the part of the Board would have done so.

Frank Laver, one of the best of good fellows, might have said, probably would have said if his temper had been more normal – for Clem Hill and Peter McAlister were not the only people who lost their tempers during the struggle – 'Well, see here, you fellows, I'm very much obliged to you; but I think this has gone far enough. There's no reason why you should all lose the trip, and Australia be short of full strength, for my sake. I am outlawed by the Board; but as for you – make your peace with it, and go!' The Board might have said: 'We are not satisfied with Mr Laver. We do not consider that he did his duty in 1909. We are the masters of Australian cricket, and we mean to remain so. But we cast no reflections on Mr Laver's probity, and if the team is determined that he shall be manager, let him be manager, though under the distinct proviso that he submits himself to our authority, and that he gives our representative every facility to exercise control over the financial part of the tour.' Not even Messrs. Hill, Armstrong and Co., could have expected the Board to accept Laver again without his making submission. But he had gone farther towards that than most people here were aware until quite lately. The books about which so much fuss was made, the books that he would not produce – those very books were taken by Clem Hill, himself a member of the Board, to a meeting of the Board – and the Board refused to have any dealing with them! Throughout, let it be distinctly understood, no charge has been made against Frank Laver's honour, in spite of the silly statements about the enormous amount paid out in tips – which was surely no one's business but that of the players, for the Board's percentage on the difference between £500 or so and, say, half the sum, is not worth mentioning.

Thus the Australian team which toured England was little more than a second eleven, though the press pointed out that it might be better to field a team united, than a team, which though stronger on paper, was full of malcontents. Some newspapers made quite vicious attacks on McAlister and implied that he was a player of no talent at all, which was not true, thus doing more harm to the cause of Hill and Laver, than good. In a protest meeting in Melbourne, McElhone, the Secretary of the Board, was described as a Nero fiddling whilst Rome was burning and McAlister was cast as Tigellinus.

Nearly all the old Australian Test Cricketers – J. W. Trumble, Joe Darling, H. H. Massie, Harry Moses, G. H. S. Trott, T. W. Garrett and W. Bruce – came down against the Board. In Hobart, T. A. Tabert, an old Tasmanian player, called for McElhone's resignation 'as he has not the confidence of the cricket-supporting public and players of Australia and his presence is a hindrance to an amicable settlement of the dispute.'

There was considerable support among the younger element for the Board and in Melbourne, Matthew Ellis, the Victorian cricketer, stood by McElhone, though when he tried to speak at a meeting he was howled down. In some quarters the original appointment of McAlister and Iredale as selectors (when Armstrong and Trumper were available) was looked upon as a deliberate plot by McElhone to bring the players to heel once and for all, and although there were a number of opportunities when the Board could have held out an olive branch and calmed the situation, they refused to make any conciliatory gestures.

On 13 March, a special meeting of the New South Wales Cricket Association was held during which a motion of no confidence in the three New South Wales delegates to the Board of Control was moved. Since one of these delegates was none other than McElhone, the meeting was looked upon as a test of the players' strength against that of the Board. In the event the no confidence motion was lost by 23 votes to 8, despite the presence of the great Victor Trumper.

The Victorian Cricket Association met to discuss the question of the Board's dealings with Laver and his account books. The action taken by the Board was endorsed by 22 votes to 2. Queensland were almost solid in favour of the Board, Western Australia sat on the fence, only South Australia was against the Board's actions. The English magazine *Cricket* got some stick for trying to maintain an impartial view:

Dear Sir – The 6 Strikers of Australia:
You have made a great mistake. Read the 'Referee'. You can't be on both sides. Is it not convincing that the Victorian Cricket Association and Laver's own Victorian club support law and order and the Board? What is a Board of Control for, but to control? For reasons which commend themselves to most people, the Board, who had the last say by the constitution intimated: 'Get someone else that we can agree to, not Laver – there are scores of others well qualified.' The Union of Players said: 'Laver or none'. So the Board says: 'None has it.' And the Six Certainties are the Sick Certainties, and the saddest man in Sydney to-day is Mr. M. A. Noble, the Chief Agitator, who on a memorable occasion traitorously deceived his own Association, and became the Keir Hardie of Cricket. Why do you find it necessary to lick the players' hands and fawn upon them? Yours, 'Old Subscriber, till now'.

And the reply from another reader:

One would expect manliness from a British Sporting paper, but the Motto is: 'Offend none: keep in with all.' I should be sorry to judge the Board of Control by this particular specimen of their supporters, who is obviously one of those who cannot understand a non-partisan attitude. To him the Board is white as the driven snow. Hill Armstrong and Co., are black as the raven. I have never been able to see things like this. There are few blacks and whites to my eyes, only various shades of grey.

In July, various people in Melbourne were making attempts to get the Victorian cricket clubs to send anti-Board delegates to the Victorian Cricket Association and thus remove the pro-Board majority. Mr McElhone was asked his views on the matter and replied that nothing the Melbourne Cricket Club did would surprise him; the Club was merely acting out of envy, since the Board of Control now had all the power which had been formerly held by the Melbourne Club. McElhone was firmly in charge, and his supporters in Sydney held a banquet in his honour at the Town Hall. The principal speaker of the evening, Sir Joseph Carruthers, said:

> Individuals were no longer allowed to control the game. That was the work of bodies appointed by the cricketers themselves. The change came not too soon. It was inevitable, and had to come, for it was order out of chaos. In workmen's parlance the guest of the evening was the 'king pin' of that organisation which had so satisfactorily assumed control of our national game, but at the same time he had behind him other members of the Board, besides others not on the Board, who had loyally supported him from one end of Australia to the other. . . . There were going to be no further difficulties in the future.

An editorial comment took the last sentence as being over optimistic. The 'revolting' players had a very strong body of public support.

The main topic of discussion was now a proposed tour by the 'revolting' players and their colleagues to America in 1913. The Board were adamant that no tours by Australian cricketers should take place without the Board's permission – if the tour went ahead ignoring the Board, would all the participating players then be banned from cricket in Australia?

What of the 1912 Australian team in England? Terrible weather in fact ruined the Triangular Test Series and most of the tour, but the team performed better than many had expected. The representative of the Board who accompanied the team however reported to his masters: 'the conduct of certain unnamed members of the team was so disgustingly bad in England that the side as a whole was socially ostracised and even the non-offenders recognised the justice of this treatment.' It was therefore recommended that in future 'the selectors should be instructed to consider other matters besides mere playing ability.' This directive has been the cause of much argument since then. Complaints on the behaviour of some members of the Australian team continued on the homeward voyage; it was alleged that two of the team were continually intoxicated on several occasions and made public exhibitions of themselves.

E. R. Mayne, the Australian Test cricketer, applied to the Board on 6 December 1912 for permission to take a team to America in 1913 – Mayne was refused permission. The *Adelaide Sporting Mail* in February 1913 carried the following comments:

> E. R. Mayne, whose batting has been a prominent feature of the season's cricket, is endeavouring to organise an Australian Eleven to visit America during the coming winter. He has made satisfactory progress, but at the present moment is awaiting final word from America, regarding the arrangements, before the team will be finally selected. It is purely a private venture, and obviously will not have any connection with the Board of Control. While it would not be possible for an Australian Eleven to go to England without the approval of the Board, there is no need to ask for that approval in connection with a trip to America. If a dozen cricketers agree to band themselves together, take a holiday in the States, and play a series of cricket matches, there is nothing in the world to stop them. Mayne has every prospect of getting together a strong combination, including some of the finest players in the Commonwealth, and cricketers will join in wishing them the best possible success in their tour. But if the projected tour is really no business of the Board's, Mayne made a distinct false step when he asked the Board for its sanction. He was refused. Now whatever he does will have been done in face of that refusal, and he and those with him must abide by the consequences. It is all very puzzling, and the dates make it even more so, for the news given in the 'Sportsman' of 6 March implied, if it did not distinctly state, the Board's consent. Until I hear that the team has actually sailed, I shall not feel sanguine that the tour will come off. Trumper, Bardsley, Macartney and Mayne will scarcely defy the Board flatly, I think; and it is very unlikely that the Board will take the same view as the 'Sporting Mail' does.

Meanwhile the players whose conduct was criticised during the 1912 England were named as W. Carkeek, T. J. Matthews and

D. Smith; the captain, S. E. Gregory, was criticised only for his lack of discipline.

The Australian newspapers were evenly divided on the question of what the Board ought to do with regard to the tour to America; either stop it before plans proceeded further, or ignore it entirely. The Board in fact ignored it.

Time was gradually dissipating the ill-feeling between the Board and the players. McElhone retired as Secretary during 1914 and the Board reinstated Clem Hill as one of the selectors for the tour to South Africa in 1914–15 – Armstrong was named as captain, so the Troubles were finally at an end. In the winter of 1914 the Melbourne Cricket Club gave up the seat it had been allocated on the Board and this place was given to the Victorian Cricket Association.

A. G. Moyes, in his *Australian Cricket – A History*, states that the bitterness did not die and that 'the Victorian scene was frequently disturbed by rumblings as of a volcano liable to erupt at any time.' Rowland Bowen, however, took the view that 'it was over before the greater thunder of the European war could be heard.' That there were quarrels between Board and players after the First World War there is no doubt – but these were of a different ilk.

5   Bodyline

The most famous of all cricket tours is that of the MCC to Australia in 1932–33. The tactics used by the England fast bowlers under the direction of a captain almost fanatical in his determination to win led to bitterness between the two countries which spread beyond cricket and caused concern to the governments. There was talk not only of cricketing relations coming to an end but of a rift in the Empire. Fifty years later the controversy surrounding the tour was enough to inspire books, articles, a play, a feature film in England and a television documentary series in Australia.

Just as the effects of this cricketing conflict can be traced in the subsequent careers of the leading actors and the conduct of the game since, it is necessary, to put its events in perspective, to look back before the tour and consider the batting and bowling conventions of the time.

The dispute centred on intimidatory bowling, which the Australian press called 'bodyline', a term so succinct and descriptive that despite the MCC's refusal to use it, or even to understand it, it became the key word in the argument.

The MCC preferred the term 'leg-theory', a type of bowling with a long and respectable history. The theory was that inswing bowlers, particularly left-handers bowling round the wicket, were naturally going to move the ball across the batsman, that a misjudged stroke would more often cause the batsman to play outside rather than inside the line of flight, and that snicks were therefore more likely to go to leg than to the off. To set a field of short legs rather than slips to accept the catches was no more than sensible. The England all-rounders G. H. Hirst and F. R. Foster used the plan successfully, Foster performing particularly

well on the tour of Australia in 1911–12. C. F. Root of Worcestershire, a right-arm inswinger, also used leg-theory effectively
in the 1920s. Even after the bodyline tour had caused the whole
question of bowling aimed at or outside the leg stump to be re-
examined, it was still in order to bowl to a 'leg-trap', and the
off-break bowler J. C. Laker was devastating with his short leg
field in the Old Trafford Test in 1956. In 1932, therefore, an
attack designed to produce catches in the short leg area was
not regarded as exceptional in itself.

Batting techniques, as well as bowling methods, were also to
come under scrutiny during the bodyline controversy. The so-
called 'Golden Age' of cricket, epitomised by dashing amateur
batsmen dominating bowlers with free-flowing off-drives off the
front foot, had ended with the First World War. Batsmen now
were accumulating runs in a more scientific and less abandoned
style. They were helped by the leg-before-wicket Law, which
required the ball to be pitched on a line between the wickets
before the batsmen could be given out. Batsmen could move
across the wicket to balls outside the off stump, with the knowledge that their pads would form a safe second line of defence
against any late movement. Further, by opening their stance
batsmen could pull the ball into the more profitable areas on
the leg side.

The most prolific of the world's batsmen as the 1932–33 tour
approached was D. G. Bradman. His career figures so exceed
all others that it is difficult to claim that he was not the best
batsman who ever lived. He had established himself in the
Australian side in 1928–29, aged 20, and had come to England
in 1930 soon after making a world record first-class score of
452 not out for New South Wales at Sydney. He went from
triumph to triumph in England, scoring 334, 254 and 252 in
Tests, with an overall tour average of 98.66. His footwork was
dazzling, and the pull to the mid-wicket boundary of balls
outside the off-stump was a favourite shot. Bradman's
supremacy was complete. He could win a Test match almost
on his own, and getting him out twice in one match was clearly
to be a problem for the captain of the 1932–33 English tourists.

That captain was to be D. R. Jardine. He had excelled at
his public school, Winchester, and had played in the Oxford

University team for four seasons, making his debut for Surrey in the second. Although not always available, he headed the English batting averages in 1927 and 1928, making his England debut in the latter year, and he toured Australia in 1928–29. In 1932, P. G. H. Fender, the popular Surrey captain, was asked to stand down so that Jardine could take over the County leadership.

Meanwhile, the year before, the MCC had chosen a Test selection committee of three – P. F. Warner, P. A. Perrin and T. A. Higson – to serve for two years and develop a side to win back the Ashes in 1932–33. Lord Hawke joined the committee as chairman before the touring side was selected, and on 4 July 1932 it was announced that D. R. Jardine would be captain. The other main contender was A. P. F. Chapman, the captain of the 1928–29 tourists, who was inferior to Jardine as a batsman. From that day on, Jardine devoted his thoughts to ways of beating Australia, which meant, to a great degree, ways of curbing Bradman.

To what extent he sought the opinions and advice of others, and what plans, if any, actually evolved before the tour, are largely matters of speculation. It has been suggested that his long-time Surrey captain, Fender, a master tactician and inno-vator, was the inspiration of the bodyline tactic. It would be unnatural if the two men had not frequently discussed the forthcoming tour. According to Fender's biography, however, the main help Fender gave Jardine was to show him letters from Australia confirming the exaggerated habit of the Australian batsmen of moving across their wicket to play the ball to leg. Fender, had, however, criticised Bradman's batting against the fast bowler Larwood on a wet wicket at the Oval in 1930, and might have strengthened Jardine's already-held view that speed was the answer to the Australians.

Much has been made of a meeting held at the Piccadilly Hotel in early August 1932 during the Surrey v Notts match, always played in those days at the Bank holidays. Present were Jardine, the Notts captain A. W. Carr, and his two fast bowlers, H. Larwood and W. Voce. Carr had captained England in four drawn games against Australia in 1926. Larwood, effectively top of the bowling averages in 1931 and 1932, and Voce were in the second batch of players picked to tour, just announced. It has been deduced by some writers that at the Piccadilly Hotel meeting the 'plan' of bodyline was laid. The only half-confirmation for this comes in Larwood's autobiography, written many years later, in which he reveals that fast bowling on the leg stump was discussed. Certainly, in Notts' next match against Essex, Larwood bowled leg-theory. This match has been described as a trial – the first in which 'bodyline' appeared. Interestingly, it did not worry the Essex batsmen, who easily forced a draw. The experiment was then repeated against Glamorgan, who also had the better of a draw, M. J. C. Turnbull hitting 205 in five hours.

Jardine also discussed leg-theory in the summer of 1932 with Frank Foster, who had practised it with success in Australia. Whatever the doubts about how far Jardine had formed his plan of attack before the 1932–33 tour, it can be said that he had decided to base it on fast bowling, and that some sort of leg-theory was part of it.

The touring party took shape in July and August. Soon after Jardine's appointment, joint-managers were announced: P. F. Warner, a member of the MCC Committee, and R. C. N Palairet, the Surrey secretary. Then W. R. Hammond, H. Sutcliffe, K. S. Duleepsinhji, L. E. G. Ames and G. Duckworth were picked. The next group were G. O. B. Allen, R. W. V. Robins, F. R. Brown, R. E. S. Wyatt, the vice-captain, H. Larwood, W. Voce and the Nawab of Pataudi. The last three selected were M. Leyland, H. Verity and M. W. Tate. Robins and Duleepsinhji dropped out, and were replaced by T. B. Mitchell and E. Paynter. Finally, W. E. Bowes was added to the side.

The late inclusion of Bowes is noteworthy. At 6ft 3in, he could make the ball rise steeply, and his use of the bumper in the previous two seasons in England had attracted criticism. His selection meant that five fast, or near-fast, bowlers were in the party – Larwood, Voce, Allen, Tate and Bowes. The addition of Bowes to an already adequate party might be seen as an indication that Jardine had considered intimidatory bowling as part of his scheme.

The party sailed on the SS *Orontes* on 17 September, played its usual match in Ceylon *en route*, and arrived at Fremantle on 18 October. All the batsmen made runs in the early games, with easy wins against South Australia and Queensland. Bradman played for a combined Australian XI at Perth, and was out cheaply. The fast bowlers were not over-extended, but all took wickets, except Larwood, who had bowled only 11 overs prior to the fifth match, against an Australian XI at Melbourne. In this match, Bradman made his second appearance against the tourists, and Larwood, Voce and Bowes were lined up against him. Jardine tested his leg-theory, progressively strengthening the leg-side field as the bowlers dropped short of a length. Voce, being a left-hander, often bowled round-the-wicket to a leg-side field in England and Bowes, as has been noted, normally bowled a proportion of bouncers. Spectators and press, however, were incensed at this first sight of 'bodyline'. Larwood, too, tried the leg-side attack and dismissed Bradman cheaply twice. He also hit W. M. Woodfull, Australia's captain, over the heart, a blow from which Woodfull took several minutes to recover. Although the best bowling figures in the match were by the Australians R. K. Oxenham, 5–53, and L. E. Nagel, a 6ft 6in swing bowler, who took 8–32 in MCC's second innings all-out 60, the English bowling strategy caused much comment in the press of the 'Is it cricket?' kind and Bradman remarked on it to the Australian Board. Woodfull's injury reminded Melbourne spectators of the match between Victoria and MCC on the previous tour. Larwood had been booed on that occasion, to the extent that the England captain Chapman had stopped the game, and Woodfull had made 275 not out.

Larwood did not play in the next match, an easy win against New South Wales. Voce continued his leg-theory and was barracked. Bradman failed again.

Bradman's scores against MCC had been 3, 10, 36, 13, 18 and 23, despite heavy scoring in other games. He had been in dispute with the Australian Board about a newspaper contract. He had become ill. On the morning of the first Test, he declared himself fit, but the Australian Board required a medical examination, and he was said to be run-down and was omitted. The Australian public was stunned and the atmosphere as the game started was a combination of disappointment over Bradman and edginess over England's bowling tactics.

In the event, the pitch was placid, but Larwood, in his third over, hit Ponsford on the hip. It was a minor incident which would have gone unremarked in normal circumstances. But the noisier sections of the crowd shouted their disapproval. Jardine calmly moved himself from gully to short fine leg. The angry spectators chanted as Larwood began his next delivery. The reaction was unjustified. Larwood bowled only four overs. His replacement, Allen, bowled as usual to the slips. Voce bowled leg-theory in his normal way and soon had Woodfull caught behind, attempting a hook. Lunch score: 63 for 1.

After lunch, Larwood began to bowl at electrifying speed, but to a full length. Ponsford was bowled leg stump, Fingleton caught at short leg, but not from a short ball, Kippax lbw: 87 for 4, Larwood 3 for 7 since lunch. Stan McCabe then launched himself into what has been accepted as one of the great innings, and the finest against bodyline. With mostly tail-end partners, he scored 187, remaining not out at the end having added 55 for the last wicket with Wall, who scored 4. But was it really bodyline? Larwood occasionally bowled to a leg-side field, but only Voce persistently bowled leg-theory. Even he was forced to abandon it, as McCabe hooked and slashed 65 runs from him. Australia scored 360, but England passed this total with two wickets down, and with Larwood taking 5–28 in the second innings, England needed only one run to win by 10 wickets.

Jardine's gesture in moving to short leg after Ponsford had been hit was typical of him. He was quite prepared to wage psychological war against the Australians. One or two earlier incidents of the tour had already singled out Jardine as the 'stage' villain, the one the Australian crowds wanted to abuse. Some Australians might have remembered the final Test of the previous tour, when Jardine, out for a duck in England's second innings, left for India and did not field in Australia's innings which took the final two days of an eight-day match. There was a haughtiness and arrogance about his character that they quickly spotted. He had a contempt for Australians which he did not disguise. Born in Bombay, where his father was a barrister, he had had a privileged education at an English public school at a time when public schoolboys were still expected to provide future administrators of the Empire. Indeed, even in 1932, Empire Day was celebrated in English schools with fancy dress parties and half-holidays. He would not be alone among his contemporaries had he regarded the Empire as a sort of English property to be patronised and subdued. He was scrupulously fair, in what he saw as fairness, but would not heed the opinions of the colonials. He was not unique. What he stood for could be recognised in MCC corridors of power before and since.

Perhaps Jardine's particular scorn of Australians had been sharpened as a student during the encounter between Oxford University and Warwick Armstrong's Australians of 1921. He was 96 not out at the end of the match which, at the Australian's request, had been cut to two days. That the Australians would not squeeze in another couple of overs so that he could score 100 no doubt struck him as uncouth.

It is not irrelevant to dwell on Jardine's character or at least the outward manifestation of it, because in the explosive atmosphere that built up as the tour progressed it contributed greatly to the anger of the Australians in the crowd. The qualities which might be admired in England – an unswerving devotion to a principle, a refusal to explain or excuse, a certain grim humour, reticence and dignity – would not cut much ice among Australians. They were goaded by the multi-coloured Harlequin cap he wore, and the silk choker he tied round his neck, symbols, they thought, of class-consciousness. His unbending patrician air, the quality of seeming to look down his nose, heightened the image.

Bradman was fit for the second Test, beginning on 30 December at Perth. Jardine probably saw the confrontation with Bradman as being the moment of truth for his speed attack. He dropped Verity, the slow bowler, and brought in Bowes. Tate, who had bowled superbly on the two previous tours, but was not quite so fast, was omitted again. The England choice of four fast bowlers – Larwood, Voce, Allen and Bowes – caused comment in the Australian press, and the Melbourne crowd was prepared for fireworks.

Before the match, Jardine asked Allen to direct his attack to a leg-side field. Allen refused and declined to bowl leg-theory throughout the tour. He was the second to show dissent over Jardine's tactics. Pataudi had earlier declined to field in the leg-trap, and had been rudely banished from Jardine's plans – after making a century in the first Test, he was not selected for the remainder. But Allen was more crucial, and Jardine would not dispense with a fast bowler, even one who would not follow instructions.

Australia batted, and Bradman was soon coming in to a rapturous welcome. No doubt attempting to establish dominance from the start he moved across his wicket before Bowes delivered the first ball to him, swung at it, and contrived to drag it on to his leg stump. He had now made 103 runs in seven innings against the tourists.

By a coincidence, Bradman doubled this aggregate in the second innings, scoring 103 not out in a total of only 191. It was masterly batting against the full might of bodyline, as it had now come to be called, at least in Australia. It was enough to win the match. Although scoring only 228 and 191, Australia dismissed England for 169 and 139 and won by 111 runs.

For a while the Australian public was content. The clamorous barracking of the first few overs of the match had lessened as Australia fought back. The series stood at one match each, Bradman was in his heaven, and his magnificent innings following that of McCabe suggested that the Australian batsmen could now come to terms with bodyline. Even Jardine was regarded with equanimity. But one thing had been overlooked. The Melbourne pitch had been slow, and had early taken spin. The selection of the Australian side had been better than England's. The medium-slow H. Ironmonger and leg-break bowler W. J. O'Reilly had been more suited to the conditions. O'Reilly was the only bowler to take five wickets in an innings, and he did it in both. The English fast bowlers, had, in fact, performed extremely well to dismiss Australia for such low totals on an unhelpful pitch, particularly as Larwood had had to leave the field with boot trouble on the first day, and was not fully operative in Australia's first innings.

Australian optimism proved to be false. The climax to the bodyline tour came in the third Test just ten days later.

England batted before a record Adelaide crowd of 40,000 and Jardine, who had suffered catcalls in the nets, opened with Sutcliffe. To the spectators' delight he was out at 4, and at 30 for 4 England were struggling. But they reached 341, and Australia's innings began on the afternoon of the second day, a Saturday. Fingleton was dismissed by Allen in the second over, and Bradman replaced him.

Larwood, with the shine still on the ball, was bowling to a conventional slip field. The last ball of the third over, his second, rose sharply and Woodfull, who had moved across his wicket, was again hit over the heart. It was eight weeks since he had suffered a similar blow at Melbourne. Woodfull dropped his bat and staggered from the crease, clearly in great distress. The crowd erupted.

In the din, Jardine said to Larwood: 'Well bowled, Harold', a remark that has received much attention since, the more charitable critics assuming that it was meant to console Larwood and imply a clear accident, rather than to congratulate him.

Jardine's next action is harder to condone. Woodfull was able to carry on, Allen bowled his second over, and Larwood began his run to deliver the first ball of his third, again to Woodfull. At this point, Jardine stopped him, and rearranged his field, setting a leg-trap. To the crowd, this had only one meaning: Woodfull was hurt, Bradman had just come in, and Jardine was now going for the kill with blatant intimidation. The mood of the spectators was now at its ugliest, and it was not helped when a ball from Larwood knocked the shaken Woodfull's bat from his hands.

Why did Jardine make this obviously provocative gesture? The answer might lie in his cussed streak, a refusal to allow an emotion of the moment to deflect him from the path of duty. His policy was to set his leg-trap when the shine had left the ball. Should he delay his plans because Woodfull had been hit accidentally? To Jardine that would have been cowardice. It would have been to submit to the intimidation of the mob. The Empire had been built by fearless men making uncompromising decisions because they were right, not because they were popular. Jardine, in fact, in his determination not to be swayed by the excitement of the crowd, was probably led to change his field an over or two earlier than usual. The shine could hardly have left the ball after four overs. Having made up his mind, to carry out his plan as ostentatiously as possible was second nature. Anything else would have been weakness.

Bradman was soon out, and McCabe followed, both caught in Larwood's leg trap, and when Woodfull was bowled by Allen, Australia were 51–4, but recovered slightly to 109–4 by the close.

That evening relations between the two sides, which, whatever the private feelings, had been formally polite, were shattered by an incident in the Australian dressing room. Pelham Warner, the England manager, who had always been uneasy about his captain's tactics, and his assistant, R. C. N. Palairet, went to enquire of Woodfull's condition. The gist of Woodfull's reply was: 'There are two sides out there. One is playing cricket, the other isn't. I have no more to say'. Warner and Palairet left in distress.

The story was leaked to the papers. This indiscretion was widely suspected to be the work of J. H. W. Fingleton, the Australian opener, who was a journalist. Fingleton, later a widely read cricket writer, always denied it, thinking at one time that Bradman, who also denied it, was the culprit. Fingleton claimed to have told Woodfull years later who the 'guilty' party really was, to be told himself that the suspicion surrounding his name had cost him a place on the 1934 tour to England. In a fascinating interview given to *Wisden Cricket Monthly* fifty years later, the Australian twelfth man, L. P. J. O'Brien, who was in the dressing room at the time of the interview, named A. F. Kippax, J. Ryder, and the fast bowler of the 1890s, E. Jones, as being also present, whereas Fingleton and Bradman weren't. Some aspects of bodyline have an Agatha Christie touch.

Whoever leaked the story stoked the wrath of the Australian press and public. Papers which had previously seen the English tactics as little more than obvious, given the presence of one great fast bowler and three other very good ones, were changing their lines. In the face of their readers' anger, it was no longer politic to point out that the Australian fast bowlers, E. A.

McDonald and J. M. Gregory, had frightened the English batsmen in 1921. Now that hostility had been expressed by the Australian captain, and reported, the press was united in its condemnation of bodyline.

When the match began again on the Monday, the crowd was like a volcano waiting to erupt, but at first the Australian batsmen played the attack well. Only one wicket fell before lunch; afterwards Ponsford, not for the first time, was bowled round his legs, giving further credence to the English diehards' view that the Australian habit of moving across the wicket was the cause of their trouble. Neither wicket was taken by Larwood, but he and Allen soon took the new ball, and another batsman was injured. Larwood bowled to W. A. S. Oldfield, the popular wicket-keeper, who had made 41 runs. The ball still had its shine, and Jardine, following his practice, was not yet employing leg-theory. Oldfield went to hook a short one, missed, and was hit sickeningly on the head. He was helped off, and took no further part.

The crowd's anger now touched its apex. O'Reilly had to force his way out to bat – it seemed that had only one spectator decided to accompany him, others would have followed, and Larwood and Jardine would have been in grave peril. But these were not the days of crowd invasions. Luckily manners were different, and some communal inhibition kept spectators off the sacred turf. It did not prevent them shouting and the game continued in a ceaseless hubbub.

Australia were dismissed, and England piled on a huge lead. Jardine, almost as if his part were written for him, took 4¼ hours over 56. He was barracked throughout, and displayed his grim humour by admitting that he was, perhaps, a little slow. Australia had no chance of scoring over 500 to win, and despite Woodfull pluckily carrying his bat for 73 not out and Bradman hitting a desperate 66, England won by 338 runs.

Surprisingly, the usual niceties were observed at the end of the match, no speeches displaying rancour. There was a misunderstanding when Warner claimed Woodfull had apologized for his dressing room remarks, but Woodfull announced that it was only an apology for the personal snub – his sentiments still stood.

It was on the fifth day of the match (Tests were played to a finish, and this lasted six days) that the Australian Board formally protested to the MCC over the English tactics. The instigator was the Secretary of the Australian Board, W. H. Jeanes, who, with a minority of the Board, was present at Adelaide. First, the English managers, Warner and Palairet, were asked to abandon bodyline. They could not give such an undertaking – it was not even thought worth putting the suggestion to Jardine. Therefore the Board members present drafted a protest to the MCC, and cabled the absent members of the Board for permission to send it. As soon as a majority was reached, the following cable was despatched on 18 January 1933:

> Bodyline bowling has assumed such proportions as to menace the best interests of the game, making protection of the body by the batsmen the main consideration.
> This is causing intensely bitter feeling between the players as well as injury. In our opinion it is unsportsmanlike.
> Unless stopped at once it is likely to upset the friendly relations existing between Australia and England.

The text was read to the Australian press immediately, so was soon the subject of discussion on both sides of the world. For a document which was to receive so much attention, it was hastily and not too well composed. The use of the newspaper term 'bodyline', with its sinister implication, was bound to rouse the indignation of the MCC and the English public in general. In reviewing the cables in *Wisden Cricketers' Almanack* the following year, when tempers had cooled, the Editor, S. J. Southerton, declined to use it, as an 'objectionable term, utterly foreign to cricket'. Then there was the allegation that England were 'unsportsmanlike'. And the last sentence sounded like a threat.

If British opinion needed hardening, the cable, described for all time in *Wisden* as 'petulant', was calculated to help. However, little help was needed. So far as the great British public was concerned, reports of the matches indicated superb bowling triumphant. Of all the experts whose opinions were sought by the papers, only one or two conceded any merit in the Australian complaint. The overwhelming view was that the Australians were squealing.

There was probably more difference among Australian opinion. The Australians had actually seen bodyline, their players had been hurt, the captain had made his famous remark. The general view was that it was 'not cricket'. But there were many who were uneasy about the cable, thinking it went too far.

There would no doubt have been more sympathy with the Australian Board's complaint had it not been for Gregory and McDonald in 1921. This pair of fast bowlers had battered the English batsmen. There were even incidents comparable to those at Adelaide: McDonald had hit L. H. Tennyson over the heart and E. Tyldesley on the head, just as Larwood had hit Woodfull and Oldfield. It was easy for Englishmen to say that Australians couldn't take their own medicine, and for some Australians to be uncomfortably aware of this charge. The difference in the two series, of course, lay in Jardine's field setting, which some read as an intent to bowl at the batsman. However, the memory of Gregory and McDonald made it harder on both sides to be wholly objective in assessing Larwood.

The Australian press were naturally anxious to elicit some support for their condemnation of English tactics from the tourists, but the party issued a statement affirming their loyalty to the captain, for which Jardine must have been grateful, knowing that Warner, Pataudi and Allen at least disapproved of his methods. It transpired afterwards there were others not entirely in favour, but they kept their views to themselves.

The MCC Committee found the Australian Board's cable easy to answer, and on 23 January 1933 cabled this reply:

We, Marylebone Cricket Club, deplore your cable. We deprecate your opinion that there has been unsportsmanlike play. We have fullest confidence in captain, team and managers and are convinced that they would do nothing to infringe either the Laws of Cricket or the game. We have no evidence that our confidence has been misplaced. Much as we regret accidents to Woodfull and Oldfield, we understand that in neither case was the bowler to blame. If the Australian Board of Control wish to propose a new Law or Rule, it shall receive our careful consideration in due course.

We hope the situation is not now as serious as your cable would seem to indicate, but if it is such as to jeopardize the good relations between English and Australian cricketers and you consider it desirable to cancel remainder of programme we would consent, but with great reluctance.

This enabled the Australian Board, in turn, to soften the tone of their first cable. They did not want the financial loss of the tour being curtailed. They had time for the full Board to consider a reply, and those who objected to the earlier cable (they did not see it before it was sent) could express their views. The second Australian cable, sent on 30 January 1933 read:

We, Australian Board of Control, appreciate your difficulty in dealing with the matter raised in our cable without having seen the actual play. We unanimously regard body-line bowling as adopted in some of the games in the present tour, as being opposed to the spirit of cricket, and unnecessarily dangerous to the players.

We are deeply concerned that the ideals of the game shall be protected and have, therefore, appointed a committee to report on the action necessary to eliminate such bowling from Australian cricket as from beginning of the 1933–34 season.

We will forward a copy of the Committee's recommendations for your consideration, and it is hoped co-operation as to its application to all cricket. We do not consider it necessary to cancel remainder of programme.

Notice the suggestion that the MCC were in ignorance of the problem, not having 'seen the actual play', and the phrase 'opposed to the spirit of cricket', which is not very different to 'unsportsmanlike'.

The MCC returned to this latter point in their cable of 2 February 1933:

We, the Committee of the Marylebone Cricket Club, note with pleasure that you do not consider it necessary to cancel the remainder of programme, and that you are postponing the whole issue involved until after the present tour is completed. May we accept this as a clear indication that the good sportsmanship of our team is not in question?

We are sure you will appreciate how impossible it would be to play any Test Match in the spirit we all desire unless both sides were satisfied there was no reflection upon their sportsmanship.

When your recommendation reaches us it shall receive our most careful consideration and will be submitted to the Imperial Cricket Conference.

The Australian Board climbed down as far as they wished to go on 8 February 1933:

We do not regard the sportsmanship of your team as being in question.

Our position was fully considered at the recent meeting in Sydney and is as indicated in our cable of January 30.

It is the particular class of bowling referred to therein which we consider is not in the best interests of cricket, and in this view we understand we are supported by many eminent English cricketers.

We join heartily with you in hoping that the remaining Tests will be played with the traditional good feeling.

There the exchange of cables rested for the time being. But it had had its repercussions in government circles. Sir Alexander Hore-Ruthven, Governor of South Australia, was in London on leave at the time of the Adelaide Test, when the first cable was sent. Messages reached him from Australia asking him to use his influence to attempt to find some solution to the threatened breakdown of relations between the cricketing bodies. He went to J. H. Thomas, Secretary for the Dominions and a cabinet minister, with the result that an MCC deputation was invited to the Dominions Office in Downing Street to discuss the affair. The Attorney-General was also present. Presumably, the MCC were asked not to rock Anglo-Australian friendship.

Meanwhile, the Australian Prime Minister, J. A. Lyons, had been approached by Warner, the England manager, through E. T. Crutchley, the head of the British Mission at Canberra.

Warner's objective was to ask Lyons to persuade the Australian Board to retract the charge of 'unsportsmanlike' bowling. He feared that unless they did so, the tour would be cancelled. Lyons saw the Chairman of the Australian Board, Dr A. Robertson, and urged him to retract.

The highest Government ministers had therefore become involved on each side, which no doubt explains the conciliatory tones of the February cables, after the aggressive ones of January.

So far as the cricket was concerned, the tour continued peacefully enough. It seemed that Adelaide had drained all emotion, and that having passed to officials the responsibility for protest, the crowd was exhausted. MCC beat New South Wales and Queensland, with Larwood doing most damage (in a cricket sense) and came to Brisbane for the fourth Test with both sides still able to win the series.

Luckily, perhaps, the wicket was easy paced. Voce was injured and could not play, and Bowes was not selected, so there was unlikely from the start to be much bodyline. That which Larwood bowled on the first day was ineffective, and he was wicketless. Australia put on 133 for the first wicket and stood at 251–3 at the close, with Bradman not out. However early next day Larwood bowled Bradman 'making room' and Ponsford round his legs again, and Australia reached only 340. England, however, collapsed, and only won a first-innings lead of 16 due to Eddie Paynter, who left hospital, where he was being treated for tonsilitis, and hit 83, putting on 92 with Verity for the ninth wicket. Although Larwood took only three wickets in the second innings, one was Bradman's, and Australia's 175 was a disappointing performance, enabling England to win the match by six wickets, and the Ashes.

There were no sour notes in the speeches and functions which followed. Jardine was congratulated all round on his captaincy, and Adelaide seemed a long time ago.

Jardine naturally would not listen to a suggestion to eschew bodyline in the last Test at Sydney (it would have implied an admission that it was not entirely fair), and Voce returned to partner Larwood in its execution. Crowd protests were minor. Larwood again bowled Bradman, but Australia totalled 435.

England passed this score by 19. Both sides dropped many catches – England put down 14 possible chances in the match. An amusing exception to this was the dismissal of Larwood, who came in as a night-watchman, scored 98, and was then caught from a big hit by Ironmonger, acknowledged as one of the poorest catchers ever to be hidden in a Test match field. Larwood was given a tremendous reception, proving that in any circumstances the Australians love a great cricketer.

In the second innings, while Bradman and Woodfull added 115 for the second wicket, Larwood broke down with a fractured toe. The incident spotlighted the degrees of ruthlessness in the make-up of the two captains. Woodfull would not take advantage of Larwood's injury as the bowler tamely completed his over; Jardine would not permit Larwood to leave the field while Bradman was batting. As soon as Bradman was out, Larwood was allowed to seek treatment in the pavilion. Australia collapsed dramatically, and England won by eight wickets, but not before Jardine had characteristically (and justifiably) complained about the follow-through onto the wicket of the fast bowler, H. H. Alexander. The apparent irony woke up the crowd, who cheered further when Jardine himself was hit – Jardine, of course, though badly hurt, disguised it as best he could. Perhaps the Sydney Hill had the last word on Jardine. Walking out to bat in complete silence, Jardine brushed away a fly from his face. 'Hey, Jardine', came a shout from the hill. 'Leave our bloody flies alone'.

The end of tour celebrations were as convivial as ever, but the Australian team did not see off the tourists, who left to play three matches in New Zealand, minus Larwood and Pataudi, who returned home alone.

The bodyline controversy was far from over as the tourists departed. In Australia, there was a determination that bodyline would not be repeated, particularly on the Australian tour of England in 1934. In England, there was a refusal to believe that the tourists had played anything but excellent cricket. Jardine and Larwood were heroes who had recovered the Ashes in the most convincing manner.

Before the party arrived home, there was a cable from the Australian Board, which had met on 21 April 1933 to consider a proposal submitted by the committee mentioned in the cable of 30 January. This sub-committee had been set up to consider a new Law, as invited by the MCC in their cable of 23 January. The latest cable ran:

> Australian Board adopted following addition to Laws of Cricket in Australia namely:–
> Any ball delivered which, in the opinion of the umpire at the bowler's end is bowled at the batsman with the intent to intimidate or injure him shall be considered unfair and 'No-ball' shall be called. The bowler shall be notified of the reason. If the offence be repeated by the same bowler in the same innings he shall be immediately instructed by the umpire to cease bowling and the over shall be regarded as completed. Such bowler shall not again be permitted to bowl during the course of the innings then in progress.
>
> Law 48a shall not apply to this Law. Foregoing submitted for your consideration and it is hoped co-operation by application to all cricket.

This was fighting talk, as the Australian Board, in the current structure of the game, were not entitled to adopt such a Law. But now the Australians could afford to attack. The next meeting of the countries would be in England, and the Board's representative in London, Dr R. Macdonald, made it clear that that tour might well be cancelled if the MCC would not agree to outlaw bodyline. This would be a bitter blow to the MCC as rulers of the game. It would also mean lost revenue, and there would be the Government itself to consider.

The MCC set up a sub-committee to consider the Australian proposal. First of all, it had to ascertain the facts of the recent tour, and interviewed the managers, Warner and Palairet, the captain Jardine, and Larwood, Voce and wicket-keeper Ames. Judged by their writings and sayings, only Warner would have supported a move to curb bodyline (which, of course, was still an emotive word, and not one the MCC Committee would sanction, as their next cable will show). Not surprisingly, the sub-committee gave more weight to the views of Jardine, and when the MCC replied to the Australian Board's cable, it rejected the new Law, stated it would seek opinions itself from the English Counties, and hit back by deprecating the barracking which Jardine's team had suffered. The cable sent on 12 June 1933 read as follows:

The MCC Committee have received and carefully considered the cable of the Australian Board of Control of April 28th last. They have also received and considered the reports of the Captain and Managers of the cricket team which visited Australia 1932–33.

With regard to the cable of the Australian Board of Control of April 28th last, the Committee presume that the class of bowling to which the proposed new law would apply is that referred to as 'body-line' bowling in the Australian Board of Control's cable of January 18th. The Committee consider that the term 'body-line' bowling is misleading and improper. It has led to much inaccuracy of thought by confusing the short bumping ball, whether directed on the off, middle or leg stump, with what is known as 'leg-theory'.

The term 'body-line' would appear to imply a direct attack by the bowler on the batsman. The Committee consider that such an implication applied to any English bowling in Australia is improper and incorrect. Such action on the part of any bowler would be an offence against the spirit of the game and would be immediately condemned. The practice of bowling on the leg stump with a field placed on the leg side necessary for such bowling is legitimate and has been in force for many years. It has generally been referred to as 'leg-theory.' The present habit of batsmen who move in front of their wicket with the object of gliding straight balls to leg tends to give the impression that the bowler is bowling at the batsman, especially in the case of a fast bowler when the batsman mistimes the ball and is hit.

The new Law recommended by the Australian Board of Control does not appear to the Committee to be practicable. Firstly, it would place an impossible task on the umpire, and secondly, it would place in the hands of the umpire a power over the game which would be more than dangerous, and which any umpire might well fear to exercise.

The Committee have had no reason to give special attention to 'leg-theory' as practised by fast bowlers. They will, however, watch carefully during the present season for anything which might be regarded as unfair or prejudicial to the best interests of the game. They propose to invite opinions and suggestions from County Clubs and Captains at the end of the season, with a view to enabling them to express an opinion on this matter at a Special Meeting of the Imperial Cricket Conference.

With regard to the reports of the Captain and Managers, the Committee, while deeply appreciative of the private and public hospitality shewn to the English Team, are much concerned with regard to barracking, which is referred to in all the reports, and against which there is unanimous deprecation. Barracking has, unfortunately, always been indulged in by spectators in Australia to a degree quite unknown in this Country. During the late tour, however, it would appear to have exceeded all previous experience, and on occasions to have become thoroughly objectionable. There appears to have been little or no effort on the part of those responsible for the administration of the game in Australia to interfere, or to control this exhibition. This was naturally regarded by members of the team as a serious lack of consideration for them. The Committee are of opinion that cricket played under such conditions is robbed of much of its value as a game and that unless barracking is stopped, or is greatly moderated in Australia, it is difficult to see how the continuance of representative matches can serve the best interest of the game.

The Committee regret that these matters have to be dealt with by correspondence and not by personal conference. If at any time duly accredited representatives of Australian Cricket could meet the Committee in conference, such conference would be welcomed by M.C.C.

Meanwhile the English season was under way. Cricketers and newspaper correspondents had endlessly analysed the winter's tour, newsreel film was being seen, and best of all, spectators and officials could judge the effect which the bodyline tour would have on the cricket of 1933.

It was considerable, and it began gradually to change English opinion. There was no opportunity to see Larwood and Voce in action, as Larwood's toe prevented him playing, and Voce took some time to return to normal hostility. Allen, although not a bodyline bowler, bowled in only three matches. It was left to Bowes to make the first impact, knocking out F. Watson of Lancashire and W. W. Keeton of Nottinghamshire, as well as hitting several other batsmen.

Then came the University match. Cambridge played the tall and extremely fast K. Farnes, a 22-year-old who had made his debut for Essex three years earlier, and was soon to play for England. Farnes' speed earned over 100 wickets that season. Against Oxford, he bowled short to a leg trap, and was altogether too much for the University players, several of whom were hit.

If this match, dear to the hearts of the 'establishment', made MCC members think, the Old Trafford Test match equally impressed the public. The West Indies were outclassed in the series, but in L. N. Constantine and E. A. Martindale they possessed two very aggressive fast bowlers. In the second Test, these two bowled to a leg trap. Hammond, emerging as England's best batsman of the 1930s, retired after taking a nasty delivery on the chin. It was typical of Jardine that he made a dogged 127. This was the only Test of the three that Constantine was available, and West Indies drew with a first-innings lead, being beaten by an innings in the others. Bodyline was therefore a profitable tactic for the West Indies, and the match made the spectators think more deeply about its implications.

A. W. Carr, the Notts captain, who, it will be remembered, had discussed leg-theory with Jardine and given it a trial against Essex, was also given cause to think further. He was a target when the Leicestershire fast bowler, H. A. Smith, incensed by the tactics of Voce, replied in kind. While Carr was prepared to use Larwood and Voce in any way the Laws allowed, it appeared that he was now joining those who wanted the Laws changed.

With the season three-quarters over, the Imperial Cricket Conference met at Lord's to discuss, among other things, the new Australian Law. By now the MCC Committee were coming to the view that something should be done about intimidatory bowling. But the mainstream of English opinion was that the Australian Law should be rejected, and it was likely that the ICC would take this line and jeopardize the Australian tour. A deferment of any decision was required, and the ICC agreed to put back the discussion until after the report of the Counties, mentioned in the cable of 12 June.

Shortly after this meeting, Voce was barracked at the Oval for his leg-theory bowling, when he several times hit the universally admired J. B. Hobbs, who was then aged 50.

During all this time, the Australian Board's representative in London, Dr A. Macdonald, was acting as a liaison between the Board in Australia and the MCC, and reporting the MCC's changing view and their desire to see the Australians touring amicably in 1934. Largely on his advice, the Australian Board's reply to MCC's previous cable was calm, and designed to allow the MCC to accommodate the Australian view without too much loss of face. Sent on 22 September 1933, it read:

> We note that you consider that a form of bowling which amounted to a direct attack by the bowler on the batsman would be against the spirit of the game. We agree with you that Leg-theory Bowling as it has been generally practised for many years is not open to objection. On these matters there does not appear to be any real difference between our respective views.
>
> We feel that while the type of bowling to which exception was taken in Australia, strictly was not in conflict with the Laws of Cricket, yet its continued practice would not be in the best interests of the game. May we assume that you concur in this point of view and that the teams may thus take the field in 1934 with that knowledge?
>
> We are giving consideration to the question of barracking and you may rely upon our using our best endeavours to have it controlled in future tours.
>
> We are most anxious that the cordial relations which have so long existed between English and Australian cricket shall continue.

The MCC's next cable, on 9 October 1933, read:

The MCC Committee appreciate the friendly tone of your cable and they heartily reciprocate your desire for the continuance of cordial relations.

In their view the difference between us seems to be rather on the question of fact that on any point of interpretation of the Laws of Cricket or of the spirit of the game. They agree and have always agreed that a form of bowling which is obviously a direct attack by the bowler upon the batsman would be an offence against the spirit of the game.

Your team can certainly take the field with the knowledge and with the full assurance that cricket will be played here in the same spirit as in the past and with the single desire to promote the best interests of the game in both countries.

The Committee much appreciate your promise to take the question of barracking into consideration with a view to ensuring that it shall be kept within reasonable bounds.

Your team can rely on a warm welcome from MCC, and every effort will be made to make their visit enjoyable.

Agreement was being reached without the MCC admitting that Jardine's tactics were culpable, or the Australian's admitting that they weren't. The Australian Board were still determined there would be no misunderstanding with their next cable, dated 16 November 1933:

We appreciate the terms of your cablegram of October 9 and assume that such cable is intended to give the assurance asked for in our cablegram of September 22.

It is on this understanding that we are sending a team in 1934.

Shortly after this the opinions of the Counties on bodyline, or fast leg-theory, were considered at Lord's. It was decided that no alteration to the Law was required. It was agreed, however, that direct attacks on the batsman by the bowlers offended the spirit of the game. It was also agreed that that matter could safely be left to the captains.

The MCC cable of 12 December 1933, still left a dangerous amount of room for continued Australian opposition:

Reference your cable of November 16th, you must please

accept our cable of October 9th, which speaks for itself, as final.

> We cannot go beyond the assurance therin given. We shall welcome Australian cricketers who come to play cricket with us next year. If, however, your Board of Control decide that such games should be deferred, we shall regret their decision.
>
> Please let us know your Board's final decision as soon as possible and in any event before the end of the year.

However, the Australian Board decided enough was enough, replying two days later:

> With further reference to your cable of October 9 and your confirmatory cable of December 12 in reply to ours of November 16, we, too, now regard the position finalised. Our team will leave Australia on March 9.

On the same day, a relieved MCC replied:

> Thank you for your cable. We are very glad to know we may look forward to welcoming the Australians next summer. We shall do all in our power to make their visit enjoyable.

It was the last of the bodyline cables, and the first to use the words 'Thank you'.

If bodyline was more or less over, at least in theory, there were big problems still to come. Would Larwood, Voce and Bowes play against Australia in 1934 and how would they bowl? Who would tell Jardine to amend his tactics?

The last cable was sent the day before Jardine, without any of these bowlers, captained England in the first Test against India at Bombay. By the end of the tour, only one of 34 matches had been lost, and Jardine topped the tour batting averages. He and Larwood were still very much the heroes of the English public, who looked forward to seeing for themselves the defeat of Australia.

Jardine was now an embarrassment. If the forthcoming Australian tour were to repair the damaged friendly relations between the countries, officials on both sides felt that Jardine could not be captain. Yet how could he be dropped?

Jardine solved this problem himself. Despite his inner

strength, the Australian tour must have been an emotional strain. He had not wished to tour India, but had been persuaded that his appointment as captain was a mark of MCC's support. Viewing matters from India and no doubt having the changing MCC opinions relayed to him, either officially or unofficially, he must have felt that this unqualified support was now being withdrawn. He stayed in India after the tour, and on 31 March 1934 announced via a newspaper that he would not play against Australia that summer. There was no word to MCC, and no reasons given. He did not play for England again, and left the Test arena with the aloofness with which he'd played.

Larwood was to be more awkward. He remained, despite his foot trouble, the bowler most likely to be able to restrain Bradman's prodigious run-getting. The selectors, among whom Sir Stanley Jackson had replaced Warner, wanted Larwood, but not leg-theory. Jackson put this to Larwood before the season began. According to Larwood, he was also indirectly approached by the selectors through Sir Julien Cahn, a Notts member who regularly took first-class sides abroad on private tours. This approach went further – Larwood should also apologize for his bowling in Australia. Not unnaturally, Larwood regarded the MCC's about-face as a kind of treachery, and declared himself unfit for the first Test. However, he bowled for Notts during the Test, and admitted later that the 'injury' was diplomatic.

Larwood's future Test career probably hinged on a match between Notts and Lancashire, after Australia had won the first Test easily. Larwood and Voce demolished Lancashire, and several batsmen were hit. The Lancashire club, of which T. A. Higson, the Test selector, was chairman, made an official complaint to the MCC about the Notts bowling, suggesting that the agreement that County captains would not countenance intimidatory bowling had been flouted. They threatened not to play Notts the following season. Larwood and Voce, and the Notts captain Carr, became convinced that this protest was part of an MCC plot to force Larwood into an agreement not to bowl leg-theory if selected for the Tests. All three made their opinions known in the newspapers. In pointing out the inconsistency in the MCC's behaviour over the whole matter,

William Clarke, who anticipated Kerry Packer by over 100 years by banding together the best cricketers of the day. His England Eleven played any side that could raise a guaranteed sum. He argued with John Wisden, the founder of the famous Cricketers' Almanack, who left Clarke to set up a rival United All-England Eleven.

Alfred Shaw, the leading bowler of his day, and a leader of the Notts strike of the 1880s.

Shaw's partner, the great batsman Arthur Shrewsbury. With James Lillywhite, he and Shaw organised four tours of Australia.

The Nottinghamshire team of 1884, during the run of four successive County Championships. It includes five of the seven strikers. From left, standing: G. Street (umpire), J. A. Dixon, H. Coxon (scorer), W. Flowers, E. Mills, E. Henty (umpire). Sitting: W. Barnes, A. Shrewsbury, A. Shaw, W. Gunn, W. Attewell. On ground: W. Wright, M. Sherwin, W. H. Scotton.

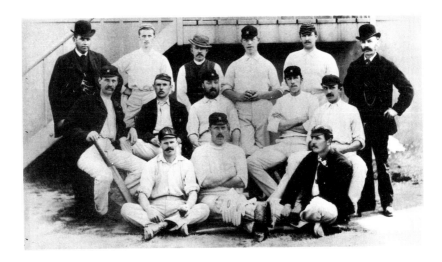

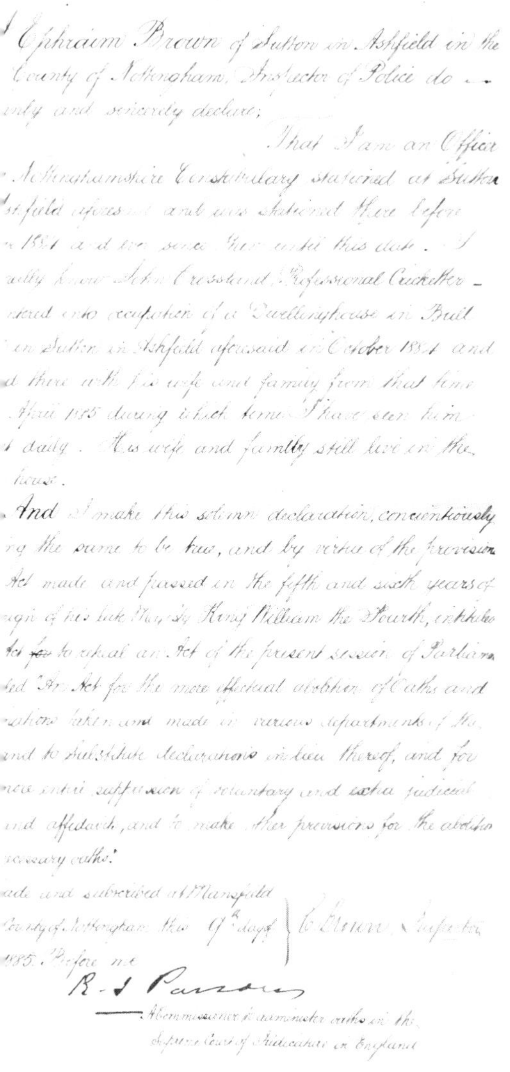

Illegal Bowling

Lord Harris, captain of Kent and England who took the law into his own hands and cancelled the Kent fixture with Lancashire because the leading Lancashire bowlers 'bowled unfairly.'

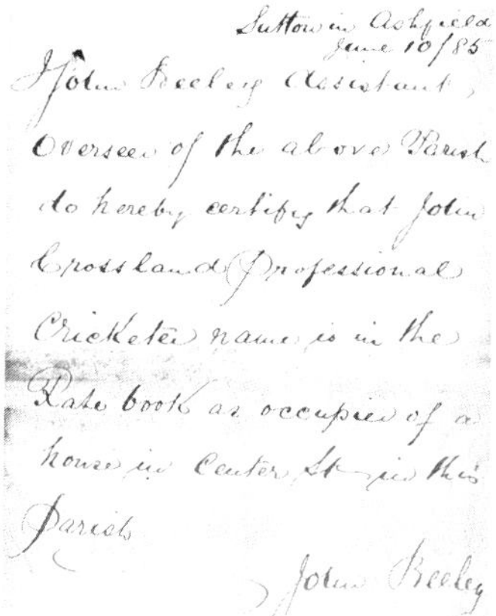

[Handwritten sworn statement, left column]

I Ephraim Brown of Sutton in Ashfield in the County of Nottingham, Inspector of Police do solemnly and sincerely declare:

That I am an Officer of the Nottinghamshire Constabulary stationed at Sutton in Ashfield aforesaid and was stationed there before ... 1881 and have since ... until this date. I fully know John Crossland Professional Cricketer ... into occupation of a Dwellinghouse in Brail ... in Sutton in Ashfield aforesaid in October 1881 and ... there with his wife and family from that time ... April 1885 during which time I have seen him ... daily. His wife and family still live in the house.

And I make this solemn declaration, conscientiously ... the same to be true, and by virtue of the provisions Act made and passed in the fifth and sixth years of reign of his late Majesty King William the Fourth, intituled ... to enact an Act of the present session of Parliament ... An Act for the more effectual abolition of Oaths and ... taken, and made in various departments of the ... and to substitute Declarations in lieu thereof, and for ... their suppression of voluntary and extra judicial ... affidavit, and to make other provisions for the abolition ... oaths.

made and subscribed at Mansfield in the County of Nottingham the ... day of ... 1885. Before me

R. S. Parsons

[signature]

A Commissioner to administer oaths in the Supreme Court of Judicature in England

[Handwritten statement, right column]

Sutton in Ashfield
June 10/85

I John Beeley Assistant Overseer of the above Parish do hereby certify that John Crossland Professional Cricketer name is in the Rate book as occupier of a house in Center St. in this Parish

John Beeley

Two of the sworn statements used by Notts in the legal battle with Lancashire over the eligibility of John Crossland, who lived in Nottinghamshire but played for Lancashire, and was ignored by England because of allegations of throwing.

THE AUSTRALIAN TEAM, 1909.

Back Row:— W. J. Whitty, A. Cotter, Roger Hartigan, V. Ransford, Warren Bardsley, H. Carter,
Second Row:— P. A. M'Alister, V. Trumper, A. J. Hopkins, M. A. Noble, Frank Laver, W. W. Armstrong, J. A. O'Con

F. LAVER. (VICTORIA)

The Australians for the tour of 1909. There was ill-feeling among the players over the choice of McAlister, a selector, as vice-captain and treasurer, and subsequent controversy over the account books. From left, standing: W. J. Whitty, A. Cotter, Roger Hartigan, V. Ransford, Warren Bardsley, H. Carter. Sitting: P. A. McAlister, V. Trumper, A. J. Hopkins, M. A. Noble, Frank Laver, W. W. Armstrong, J. A. O'Connor. On ground: S. Gregory, C. G. Macartney, W. Carkeek.

Left Frank Laver, the team manager, who kept an account book of the tour, but according to McAlister, a selector and the treasurer, would not show it to him.

Peter McAlister (**left**), was a controversial member of the Australian selection committee, who played often for Australia when a selector. Clem Hill (**right**) was the Australian captain in 1911–12, and also a selector. McAlister and Hill came to blows while picking the team for the fourth Test.

Bill Woodfull (**right**) tosses and Douglas Jardine (**left**) calls. Jardine, as Engla
captain, was primarily responsible for England's 'bodyline' tactics in 1932–3
while Woodfull, twice struck over the heart, was a principal victim, and ma
his feelings known.

Above Harold Larwood, with wife and daughter, and Bill Voce, standing behind Mrs Voce, being seen off at Nottingham station on 16 September 1932 on their way to join the England cricketers for the tour to Australia. They were to be the two fast bowling 'villains' of 'bodyline'.

Right Bert Oldfield, whose injury when struck on the head by a ball from Larwood led to the first cable to the MCC alleging 'unsports-manlike' tactics.

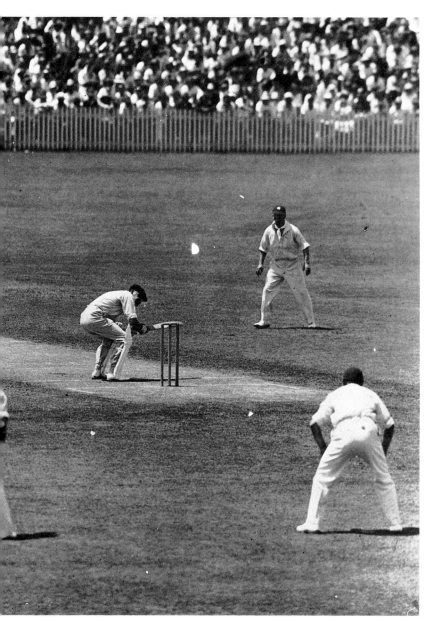

Woodfull ducks beneath a ball from Larwood during the fourth Test at
Brisbane in 1932–33. Note the ring of six short legs, the typical 'bodyline' field.

Four of the bowlers at the heart of the throwing controversies in the 1950s and 1960s. **Left** Cuan McCarthy, the South African Test bowler, whom umpire Frank Chester was told not to call as it would be undiplomatic. **Above** Australian Ian Meckiff, whose action was resented by the MCC tourists of 1958–59, and who retired after being called in South Africa. **Below** Tony Lock of England, who was called in the West Indies after bowling Sobers. **Right** Geoff Griffin of South Africa, who was called at Lord's and forced to bowl under-arm, when he was called again.

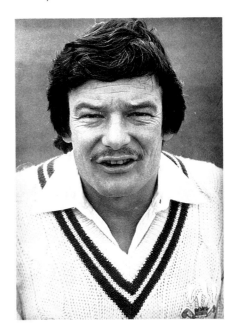

Left: Basil d'Oliveira, whose selection as a replacement for the tour of South Africa in 1968–69 caused great controversy and led to the tour being cancelled.

Right Robin Jackman, who, as a member of the England touring party in 1980–81, was expelled from Guyana for having played in South Africa. The entire party left and the Test match was cancelled.

Below Lawrence Rowe, the captain of the first West Indian team ever to tour South Africa. The secretive departure of the 'rebel' team in 1983 caused an outcry in the West Indies.

Right Lord Hawke, who in the
1880s 'took over' Yorkshire, and
established a style of autocratic rule
that lasted, in some ways, until the
1970s.

Below Brian Sellers (in blazer), the
last of the great authoritarian
Yorkshire captains, giving a pep talk
to younger members of the team.
On the left is future England bowler,
Johnny Wardle, whose dispute with
Yorkshire led to his losing his place
on a tour to Australia and his
retirement when in his prime from
first-class cricket. The story,
coupled with the earlier departure of
Test batsman Willie Watson,
caused a sensation in 1958 and was
the first of the modern Yorkshire
rows to become a public issue.

Left Brian Close, the 'Wonder Boy' of 1949 and a successful Yorkshire and England captain, was asked in 1970 by Brian Sellers, Chairman of the Cricket Committee, to resign or be sacked. An Action Group was formed and the Yorkshire Committee defeated at the AGM of 1971.

Below Yorkshire's John Player Trophy in 1983. Ray Illingworth, another Yorkshire and England captain (holding the trophy) left the County after a bitter dispute with Sellers in 1968, but returned to manage and captain the side in the 1980s. The supporters of Geoff Boycott (right), another sacked captain, forced the Yorkshire Committee to resign in 1984.

Kerry Packer (**left**), whose signing of many of the world's leading cricketers in 1977 to play in World Series Cricket shocked the authorities and threatened to disrupt the whole structure of the game. The England captain, Tony Greig (**right**) was his chief lieutenant. They are seen before the Law Courts, where they successfully challenged the new rules of the Test and County Cricket Board, which proposed restraints on the Packer players.

Larwood announced that he would not play in the remainder of the Test matches, and neither he nor Voce was selected.

As Australia went on to win the series 2–1, with a massive win at the Oval, the bodyline dispute switched to Nottinghamshire. The County match with the Australians took place in August, before the final Test. Carr and Larwood were suffering from injuries, but Voce played, and took 8–66 as the Australians, without Bradman, were dismissed for 237. Voce bowled his usual leg-theory, and the Australians were patently aggrieved. Beginning their second innings towards the end of the second day, the Australians faced two overs from Voce of fierce bumpers, which, so far as the Australians were concerned, were nothing short of a continuation of bodyline tactics. Bad light then stopped play.

The Australian management immediately made a protest to the MCC, and next day the Notts secretary announced that Voce had retired from the match with sore shins. The Nottinghamshire crowd assumed that Voce's withdrawal was as diplomatic as that of Larwood from the first Test. As they saw it, Larwood and Voce had been removed from the firing line because of Australian pressure, weakly and treacherously backed first by the MCC and now by the Notts management. The barracking which the Australians had faced on the first two days of the match was increased, and the final day was punctuated by cacophonous booing.

There was a final bodyline incident that season, at Lord's, when the Middlesex batsmen suffered at the hands of Notts, and B. L. Muncer, a newcomer to the Middlesex side, was knocked out by a Voce delivery. Middlesex followed Lancashire's lead and threatened not to play Notts the following season. (It is interesting to recall that the same three Counties were making similar threats over illegal bowling in 1885, as an earlier chapter showed).

The MCC now decided to act against dangerous bowling, under whatever name it might be described, and two important changes were incorporated into the Laws for the 1935 season. One was that lbw decisions could be given where balls pitched outside the off stump, provided the batsman was between the wickets (similar to the Law of today). The other was that umpires were instructed to prevent intimidatory bowling at batsmen standing clear of their wickets. The first change removed some of the attraction of 'leg-theory' – indeed had it been the Law in 1932–33 it might well have made Jardine's tactics unnecessary. The second did not admit that Jardine's tactics were outside the spirit of the game, as it would still be legitimate to bowl at a batsman standing or moving in front of his wicket. The current Law is more severe, merely allowing the umpire to intervene whenever he considers the bowling is designed to intimidate the striker.

In effect, this saw the end of the bodyline controversy. However, it left its marks on individuals.

In Nottinghamshire, Carr was dropped as captain and there was a furore when it became public knowledge that the Committee had apologized to MCC, and by extension to Australia, over Voce's two overs in the match against the Australians. At an Extraordinary General Meeting forced by Carr, a vote of no confidence in the Committee was passed, and the entire Committee was forced to resign. This was eventually reversed at the AGM, but only when it became clear that Nottinghamshire were in danger of being removed from the County Championship. In the end, Nottinghamshire agreed to accept the Law concerning intimidatory bowling, although the resentment of the Notts members over the actions of the MCC remained.

Carr did not play for Nottinghamshire again, and made only one more first-class appearance. Larwood bowled for Notts in 1935 at medium pace from a shortened run. He gradually regained his old prowess, and, despite suffering occasional breakdowns, was extremely effective in 1936, when he took over 100 wickets and once more effectively topped the averages. However, he did not play for England again after the 1932–33 tour. Voce bowled well in 1935, without his previous aggression. Nevertheless, despite often being let down by his slip fielders, he took 139 wickets and headed the Notts averages. He indicated his willingness to play for England in 1936, and was chosen to play against the Indians. He was then selected to tour Australia in 1936–37 under G. O. B. Allen, but to placate Australian opinion was required by Allen to apologise for his bowling on the previous tour. Voce proved to be the most effective bowler in the party. He toured Australia again in 1946–47, but by then was well past his best. Bowes continued to bowl for England, in an orthodox manner, until the war, although he was not selected for a second tour. After suffering ill-health as a prisoner of war, he played two seasons for Yorkshire afterwards.

Bodyline claimed its victims then, apart from those batsmen hit. Jardine and Larwood, the two principal heroes of 1932–33, had their Test careers curtailed, Larwood, indeed, never playing for England after the bodyline tour. Carr also had his career terminated.

In 1947 Larwood emigrated to Australia, where despite bodyline, he had always been regarded with respect and esteem. It is notable that Oldfield, whose injury at Adelaide was the last incident before the storm broke, admitted immediately that the accident was his own fault. In his autobiography, published in 1954, he described Larwood as 'a likeable fellow of retiring disposition.' Oldfield and Woodfull, the batsmen most severely hit, both continued their Test careers successfully.

Larwood was the main sufferer of the whole bodyline story, and Oldfield's words are the best with which to leave it.

In post-war years, an Indian batsman has suffered a fractured skull, a New Zealand batsman has been given the kiss of life on the pitch, an Indian captain has declared prematurely to save his tail-enders the possibility of injury, an Australian fast bowler has said his bouncers are meant to hit batsmen in the ribs, and two England batsmen near the ends of their careers have been subjected to an evening burst of West Indian bumpers which must have been at least as venomous as those bowled by Voce to the Australians in 1934. All these incidents caused excited comment, but are parts of other stories, none of which could equal the conflict caused by 'bodyline'.

6   Illegal Bowling Revived

Between the two World Wars not a single bowler was no-balled for throwing in English first-class cricket. This total absence of bowlers transgressing the Law continued until 1952, when suddenly three bowlers were 'called'. The three bowlers were Insole, Lock and McCarthy. Insole, the Essex captain and England batsman, was no more than a very occasional bowler at best and therefore his being no-balled during the Northants v Essex match at Northampton was of little consequence. Lock and McCarthy however, were fish of a very different persuasion.

Tony Lock, a left-arm slow or medium pace bowler, had gained a regular place in the Surrey side of 1950, taken over 100 wickets in 1951 and by 1952 had, in terms of figures, developed into the leading left-arm spin bowler in England. There was some debate about the legality of his bowling when he produced a faster delivery, but the England selectors chose him for the third Test of 1952 at Old Trafford and on this, his debut for England, he took 4 for 36 during the second innings, not having bowled in the first – that was on 17, 18 and 19 July. On 26 July he was playing for Surrey against the Indians at the Oval and was no-balled for throwing by Price, the old Middlesex and England wicketkeeper. Price 'called' Lock three times. The Oval crowd greeted the umpire's move with catcalls and boos.

The Laws of Cricket had been completely revised by the MCC in 1947, but the Law regarding 'throwing' remained very much as it had been proposed by Lord Harris nearly seventy years before; the 1947 version read:

> For a delivery to be fair the ball must be bowled, not thrown

or jerked; if either Umpire be not entirely satisfied of the absolute fairness of a delivery in this respect, he shall call and signal 'No-Ball' instantly upon delivery.

Price having no-balled Lock, the immediate question was, how would the England selectors react? They gathered to choose the team for the fourth Test only days after the Surrey v Indians match. To further complicate their thoughts, the Test was to be played on Lock's home ground. In the absence of someone of Lord Harris's calibre – his Lordship had died in 1932 – the selectors ignored Price and retained Lock for the Test. In the event, the match was ruined by rain and the young spin bowler was called upon for only six overs.

The other major offender of 1952 was the Cambridge University fast bowler Cuan McCarthy. Although he had only gone up to Cambridge in the autumn of 1951, he was an established South African Test player, having appeared in fifteen matches for his country, including all five Tests in England in 1951. In that series he was easily the fastest South African bowler, but very expensive. A typical newspaper comment noted: 'The England opening batsmen, Hutton and Ikin, were severely bruised during the course of the 11 overs delivered by McCarthy. He persistently sent down short-pitched bumpers. South Africa might have done better if McCarthy had paid more attention to length and direction.'

McCarthy was no-balled by umpire Corrall, the former Leistershire wicketkeeper, during the Cambridge v Worcestershire match at Worcester in June. Despite this he played in the University match at Lord's and, more interestingly, was selected by the MCC to play for the Gentlemen v Players at Lord's three weeks later. Frank Chester had stated during the 1951 Test Series v South Africa that he considered McCarthy's action unfair, but was told that it would not be diplomatic to call him.

Not only were the umpires ignored in both cases in 1952, but the cricket authorities directly challenged Price and Corrall by choosing Lock and McCarthy for representative matches almost immediately after their bowling actions had been condemned. This shilly-shallying was to prove fatal for there now began a decade of controversy. The *Wisden* Editorial covering the 1952 season was quite outspoken however:

> It was stated that the umpires concerned, who took this action when standing at square-leg, would report the facts to MCC but so far there has been no indication that the rulers carried the matter further . . . in the interests of cricket I congratulate both Price and Corrall for their efforts to see the game is conducted properly . . . Possibly a solution to the problem of dealing with throwing would be the appointment by the MCC before each season of a small panel to which umpires could report suspicious cases.

The English season of 1953 passed without any repetition of the incidents regarding throwing, the authorities seemingly more concerned with the problem of 'fast short-pitched balls at the batsman'. Throwing was soon to recur, this time in the explosive atmosphere of the West Indies. MCC, under Len Hutton, toured West Indies in the winter of 1953/54 and on the fourth day of the First Test at Kingston, Jamaica, umpire Burke no-balled Lock. A report noted: 'All the England players in the field looked up in surprise when it happened.' The following week Lock was no-balled in Bridgetown by umpire Harold Walcott, uncle of the famous Test batsman. Walcott actually called 'No-ball' after a particular delivery had clean bowled Gary Sobers. Lock protested to Hutton, but Hutton made it clear that the decision was one for the umpire and the England captain could not over-rule the official.

The standard of umpiring in the West Indies during this series came under much criticism and the MCC requested in British Guiana that the umpires appointed for the Georgetown Test be changed – MCC in fact requested the appointment of Harold Walcott, but since he came from Barbados and there was much rivalry between the various West Indian colonies, there was no hope of Walcott being chosen to stand in British Guiana.

Lock ceased bowling his faster delivery after the Bridgetown match and was not 'called' again, but his effectiveness was much reduced. In 1954 Lock was not chosen to play for England and the only bowler to fall foul of the umpires was a young

Worcestershire fast bowler, D. B. Pearson, who appeared only once in 1954 in Championship cricket.

The MCC toured Australia and New Zealand in 1954–55; Lock was not in the party, and the two fast bowlers, Tyson and Statham, had exemplary actions, as did the leading Australians. There was a short lull in the throwing rows, but ominously the next examples came in first-class domestic cricket in Australia and in South Africa. The Australian offender was Keith Slater, who was no-balled when playing for Western Australia in 1957–58. In the following season of 1958–59 there was a storm of protest over the actions of not only Slater, but Burke, Meckiff and Rorke.

The MCC side under Peter May met Western Australia for the opening first-class game of their 1958–59 tour. Keith Slater for the home side took 4 for 33 with 'his ugly baseball pitcher's action'. In the match against Victoria, MCC met Meckiff for the first time; Crawford White commented in the *News Chronicle*: 'Australia's Test left-arm pace bowler Ian Meckiff, whose bowling arm is so kinked that I still think he throws many deliveries . . .' Crawford White continued his criticism when the first Test was played at Brisbane: 'If Meckiff is not no-balled before the series is over it will be a travesty of the Laws of cricket.' Ian Peebles picked up a comment from the crowd, after one of Meckiff's more erratic spells: 'Put Harvey on. At least he can throw straight.' (This reference was to Neil Harvey, the brilliant Australian cover fielder.)

The Australian selectors caused more ill-feeling by picking Slater for the second Test. John Clarke of the London *Evening Standard* hit out: 'Slater's ugly, near-throw has caused much comment this season.' Crawford White added: 'Usually the Australian selectors demand impressive figures, or outstanding promise, but Slater has neither recommendation. He is a tall youngster, extraordinary because he bowls with his legs so bent that he delivers almost off his knees. And his right arm is so bent that he blatantly throws the ball.'

The whole problem was dealt with in *The Sunday Times*:

Rather more than two months ago several of us correspondents, English and Australian, were having a nice gentle net among ourselves at Perth. Presently we were joined by a stranger, a young man who might just have left school. As there were several veterans and rather brittle arms among us we were very glad of his assistance and the fact that his action was a blatant throw caused little comment from the other performers. It did not go un-noticed among the spectators at the back of the net where a group of small boys raised piercing cries of 'Throw' and 'No-ball'. It was not until a later stage in the trip that I began to wonder if he was not a sympton of a dangerous and rather widespread malaise in these parts. In every State we have visited we have either seen first-hand or heard of at least one action which has attracted some adverse comment. . . . Before examining particular cases, it is only proper to say that it is improbable that the offender in any case is aware of the infringement until it is brought to his notice by helpful friends, or the umpire's stentorian intervention. On our side, we have the case of Lock, whose fast ball was long suspect and was eventually 'called' in the West Indies. Since then he has satisfied a great number of competent umpires. Here in Australia we struck a very doubtful action straight away in the case of Slater at Perth. All manner of rumours flew around that he had been forced to give up fast bowling for slow off breaks because of frequent judicial interference, but these boiled down in fact to one no-ball called when he was bowling slow. Victoria have Meckiff, whose action is certainly not completely orthodox though pleasing in many ways. Many bluntly state that he throws and if the law is to be more rigorously enforced he will have to modify his delivery. In New South Wales Rorke is a splendid figure of a fast bowler and mighty quick, but his final heave is marred by the same bend and snap. His colleague, Burke, makes little pretence of bowling, but is good-naturedly accepted by all. At Brisbane last week a friend in the outer tossed him a helpful bit of advice. 'Bowl him one for a change, Burkie,' bawled his cobber, 'You'll surprise 'im.'

Jack Fingleton, the old Australian Test batsman, was as critical as the English reporters, but he was also quite certain that

Lock's faster delivery was still a 'throw', and said so when the English correspondents said Meckiff and company would be no-balled out of the game if they ever came to England.

Australia duly won the Ashes by four matches to nil and Meckiff topped the Australian bowling averages. There was not a single instance of a bowler being no-balled for throwing during the tour.

Just as the MCC team was leaving Australia, the authorities – in fact an MCC Sub-Committee – recommended that the first-class umpires should meet and draw up a list of 'doubtful' bowlers. The chief offenders in England were named as Lock and his Surrey colleague, Loader. The MCC agreed that there was no necessity to alter the wording of the Law and the umpires unanimously concurred. It was thought in 1959 that the great 'test' of the umpires strength in this matter would come in 1961, when Australia were due to tour England once again.

Meanwhile, the Australian Board of Control held demonstrations and trials in Sydney and Brisbane. They decided that the words 'or jerked' should be deleted from the Law and issued the following experimental Law:

For a delivery to be fair the ball must be bowled, not thrown: if either umpire be not entirely satisfied of the absolute fairness of a delivery in this respect, he shall call and signal 'No-Ball' instantly upon delivery. The umpire at the bowler's wicket shall call and signal 'no-ball' if he is not satisfied that at the instant of delivery the bowler has at least some part of one foot behind the bowling crease and within the return crease, and not touching or grounded over either crease.

Note 7. A ball shall be deemed to have been thrown if immediately prior to the delivery of the ball the elbow is bent, with the wrist backward of the elbow, and the arm is then suddenly straightened as the ball is delivered. This definition of a throw does not debar the bowler from any use of the wrist in delivering the ball. Umpires are particularly directed to call and signal 'No-Ball' unless they are satisfied the ball is bowled. The bowler shall not be given the benefit of the doubt.

Note 8. The difficulty confronting the umpire of simultaneously watching a bowler's hand and foot to determine 'the
instant of delivery' is realised. Should the umpire consider a
bowler is transgressing Law 26 by 'dragging' over the
bowling crease before delivering the ball, the umpire shall
request the bowler to place his back foot in the delivery stride
such a distance behind the bowling crease, that it will, in the
umpire's opinion, offset the advantage the bowler would
otherwise gain. Umpires would use a white disc to mark the
place behind which the bowler must land his back foot in
his delivery stride.

In November 1959, the MCC decided to remove the words 'or
jerked' and add the following note to the Law:

A ball shall be deemed to have been thrown if, in the opinion
of either umpire, there has been a sudden straightening of
the bowling arm, whether partial or complete, immediately
prior to the delivery of the ball. Immediately prior to the
delivery of the ball will be taken to mean at any time after
the arm has risen above the level of the shoulder in the
delivery swing. The bowler will not be debarred from the use
of the wrist in delivering the ball.

During the season of 1959, Lock was again no-balled for
throwing, while two other offenders were D. B. Pearson and
K. J. Aldridge, both from Worcestershire.

South Africa were the tourists to England in 1960 and
brought in their team Geoffrey Griffin, a fast bowler from
Natal, who had already been no-balled twice for throwing in
the 1958/59 season, but had escaped censure in 1959/60. Even
as the tourists practised at Lord's before the tour opened in
earnest, the press noted: 'Geoffrey Griffin, the South African
bowler, who may be causing English umpires, as well as English
batsmen, more than a little concern during the coming
season . . .'

In the second first-class game of the tour, the storm broke —
at Derby. It was not Griffin who fell foul of the umpires though.
Harold Rhodes, the Derbyshire fast bowler, was no-balled six
times by Paul Gibb, the former Yorkshire, Essex and England

batsman-wicketkeeper. The Derbyshire captain, Donald Carr, switched Rhodes to the other end, where he was under the jurisdiction of Ron Aspinall and was not again called. Griffin, however, bowled in this match for the tourists without any adverse comment, except from the spectators.

Donald Carr decided that the only way to solve the problem of Rhodes' bowling action was to film him and send the evidence to MCC for their consideration. Rhodes was not the only early victim of the umpires' purge. Lock was called by Arthur Fagg during Surrey's opening match of the year against Cambridge at Fenner's. Aldridge, the Worcestershire seamer, was called by Jack Crapp during the first Worcester County game.

The third South African match was at Ilford against Essex. The crowd called at Griffin 'bowl – not throw,' but umpires John Langridge and Charles Elliott made no comment. Crawford White in the *News Chronicle* stated:

> I must say that in my view, and I watched him from several angles, this fair-headed youngster seemed to throw as blatently as Australia's Ian Meckiff ever did. Perhaps our umpires, with a high degree of special courtesy, are giving the benefit of the doubt to our visitors. Or maybe the attitude is that until our own house is completely in order it would be indelicate to call a tourist.

The public and the cricket correspondents waited for the first visit of the South Africans to Lord's – a match v MCC on 21 May. This time the umpires acted and Griffin was no-balled simultaneously by umpires John Langridge and Frank Lee for both throwing and dragging – this latter offence, though overshadowed by the throwing controversy, was causing umpires headaches at the time.

Griffin was also no-balled for throwing five times during the match with Notts at Trent Bridge. Keith Miller, the former Australian all-rounder, wrote:

> The more I see of the throwing row over Geoff Griffin, the more I see the funny side. He was in trouble again at Trent Bridge yesterday when he opened the South African bowling. The first over went through without incident. The Test

umpire Jack Bartley, at square leg, called him for throwing successive balls in the second over. Griffin bowled another over – unchallenged – before skipper Jackie McGlew took him off. I could not detect one solitary delivery different in action to any other Griffin bowled in the three overs. So how Bartley sifted out these two so-called throws is beyond my cricketing knowledge. I say the umpire should either have called all the deliveries illegal or allowed them to pass – depending on how he interprets the controversial throwing law. To single out two deliveries in 18 is a joke. The more I see of Griffin the less I think he infringes this much-discussed throwing law. And in recent years I have seen such Australian shockers as Jimmy Burke and Ian Meckiff. Let's be fair, I say that Meckiff's fastest one is a straight-out 'chuck'. There is no question in my mind about it. But Griffin? He's a harmless bowler when I reflect back on the unchecked Aussies.

Griffin went to Alf Gover's Cricket School, and the old England and Surrey fast bowler and now well-known coach pronounced himself satisfied that he had 'straightened out' Griffin's bowling action. Certainly Griffin bowled 18 overs in the match at Cardiff against Glamorgan without being no-balled by either umpire. He played in the first Test at Edgbaston. The cartoonists had a field day, with Roy Ulyett suggesting that in place of the traditional 1,000 runs in May feat, there ought to be an umpires' table for 1,000 no-balls in May. The umpires were also reported to be gargling on a mixture of three parts iron filings to one part gravel, so that their voices would stand up to a full day's shouting. Griffin bowled 21 overs in each innings of the Test, picking up 4 wickets for 105, and was given a clean sheet by both John Langridge and W. E. Phillipson, two very experienced former cricketers.

In the game against Hampshire however, he was no-balled once more and John Clarke in the London *Evening Standard* then previewed the second Test at Lord's:

Over the second Test, which starts at Lord's tomorrow, hangs a great question-mark. And to the South Africans the curve of the mark of Interrogation must seem more like the blade of a scimitar poised over the game, a scimitar that may easily drop and cut off their hopes of success. The question? Will Geoff Griffin pass the scrutiny of umpires Frank Lee and Syd Buller. Or will his 'new' action again be questioned and will he be called for throwing as he was again only yesterday. South Africa's captain, Jackie McGlew, and their manager, Dudley Nourse, both declare, whenever the question crops up – and it crops up often enough in all conscience – that they and Griffin's team-mates are firmly convinced this young bowler's action is fair. They are entitled to their view and no doubt they hold it sincerely. But a growing number of observers incline to the other opinion – that Griffin's action is, more often than not, illegal. Six umpires have now no-balled Griffin, and they include Frank Lee. What makes matters worse is that two umpires now have called the bowler since his cricket school corrective course.

England batted first in the Lord's match, but, marred by rain and bad light, the first day's play lasted less than three hours. Frank Lee no-balled Griffin five times, but on the second day Griffin caused quite a sensation – by being no-balled another six times and also by achieving the first hat-trick ever in a Test at Lord's. Griffin had Mike Smith, the Warwickshire batsman, caught behind the wicket off the final ball of one over and then dismissed Peter Walker and Fred Trueman off the first and second balls of his next over. The newspapers had a field-day on this strange situation. The general consensus of opinion was that MCC were determined to make an example of Griffin because it would warn Australia not to bring Meckiff to England in 1961. The other point that was repeatedly made was that Griffin had a bent arm due to a horseriding accident and that he didn't straighten his arm just prior to the delivery of the ball.

England won the second Test with an innings to spare and to amuse the crowd on the Monday afternoon – the game having ended about half past two – the captains agreed to an exhibition game. Keith Miller's report in the *Daily Express* puts the situation graphically:

> It's crazy! Farcical! Unbelievable! Umpire Sid Buller calls
> Geoff Griffin for throwing in a carefree exhibition match

here at Lord's . . . Buller, standing at square leg, staggered even the most august MCC members by calling Griffin who ambled up from a five-yard run and rolled his arm over at half speed. 'I can't believe it,' they protested to me as Buller intimated to the cricketing world that Griffin threw. Umpire Buller watched Griffin bowl one ball from square leg. Griffin was not called. Buller then stationed himself at point. Again Griffin bowled unchecked. Buller then crossed back to square leg and in the next delivery called Griffin for throwing. He repeated the call for the next two balls. Skipper Jackie McGlew hastened over from second slip to hear Buller suggest that Griffin bowl underarm. Then Griffin underarmed and umpire Frank Lee called him because he had not notified the batsman that he intended to bowl underarm.

The South African newspapers devoted much space to Syd Buller's action and attacked both the umpires and the British press. The South African cricket authorities decided that Griffin would not bowl again on the tour.

The Australian press almost unanimously condemned Buller, with Lindsay Hassett stating:

> Of the Lord's incident, I can say without hesitation that umpire Buller's action in no-balling Griffin . . . has no parallel in my memory for presumptuous ignorance of the spirit of cricket. Commonsense interpretation of cricket law is essential . . . Those very words, in my opinion, debar Buller from ever again officiating at a first-class fixture.

Meanwhile the representatives of world cricket were gathering in London for a meeting of the Imperial Cricket Conference. Australia sent their President, W. J. Dowling, and Sir Don Bradman. The Conference re-affirmed the decision taken the previous year and recommended the following experimental definition:

> A ball shall be deemed to have been thrown if, in the opinion of either umpire, the bowling arm having been bent at the elbow, whether the wrist is backward of the elbow or not, is suddenly straightened immediately prior to the instant of delivery.

The bowler shall nevertheless be at liberty to use the wrist freely in the delivery action.

At the Advisory County Cricket Committee meeting a fortnight later the Counties agreed to a truce in matches against the Australians, but not in the County Championship.

The West Indies toured Australia in the season of 1960–61. The Test series between the two countries created a sensation from the start with the famous 'tied Test'. Meckiff played in two Tests, but was so unsuccessful – two wickets for 234 runs – that his action was ignored. Of the other doubtful Australian bowlers nothing was seen in the Tests. The team which was chosen by the Australian selectors to tour England in 1961 therefore omitted all the controversial bowlers on the grounds of lack of form. Ron Roberts noted in the *Daily Telegraph*: 'Australia's selectors have made the first gesture towards a happy tour of Britain this summer by omitting these bowlers with suspect actions.' The only bowler to offend the umpires in 1961 was Harold Rhodes of Derbyshire. He was reported during the first weeks of the season and taken out of the County side whilst his action was re-examined and modified to the satisfaction of the County authorities. In August, however, he was no-balled by Paul Gibb during the Northants match at Derby. The Derby captain, Donald Carr, took Rhodes off and subsequently bowled him at the other end, where Arthur Jepson officiated and allowed him to continue.

The situation outside England however, remained somewhat murky. Griffin continued to play for Natal and was no-balled for throwing both in 1961–62 and 1962–63. Ian Meckiff was finally no-balled in Australia, playing for Victoria in two matches in 1962–63. The West Indies had Charlie Griffith, from Barbados, who was regarded as one of the fastest bowlers in the world. He was no-balled for throwing for Barbados against the Indian touring team in 1961–62.

Meckiff's first-class career came to a dramatic end in December 1963. He was picked for Australia against South Africa for the first Test at Brisbane. Australia batted first and were not dismissed until the middle of the second day. McKenzie bowled Australia's first over and then Meckiff came on for the second. Umpire Egar no-balled Meckiff four times in that over. The crowd yelled and booed its disapproval, but the Australian captain, Richie Benaud, had little option but to take Meckiff off immediately. At the close of play a section of the crowd carried Meckiff shoulder high off the field, but the fast bowler saw that he had little future in Test cricket and announced his retirement from the first-class game.

The main problem of throwing was still not entirely solved. At a meeting at Lord's, which coincided with Meckiff being no-balled, the Board of Control decided to operate a truce on throwing for the first month of the 1964 season in all first-class matches – the umpires to report cases of 'doubtful' bowling to MCC but not call the bowler during the match. The Australians, who were to tour England in 1964, were asked their opinion and decided against a truce. The tour party in fact did not include any of the well-known 'chuckers' – Keith Slater continued to bowl for Western Australia and was to be no-balled in 1964–65, but the other main offenders had now disappeared. The only instance of an Australian being no-balled for throwing during the 1964 season occurred at Cardiff, where John Langridge called Ian Redpath. Redpath was the opening batsman and was brought on to bowl only during the closing session of the match when the serious cricket was over.

Harold Rhodes continued to have trouble with his action. He was no-balled by Syd Buller playing for Derbyshire v South Africans at Chesterfield in 1965, and it was freely rumoured that he would have been picked for England against South Africa but for the problem of his action. Derbyshire temporarily withdrew him from the County team after the South African game, but later restored him and he ended the season at the head of the first-class averages with 119 wickets, av. 11.04.

The last occasion in the 1960s when a bowler was no-balled for throwing was in 1966. The guilty party was Charlie Griffith, the West Indian fast bowler. Griffith had been no-balled in 1961–62 in the West Indies, but in 1963 he had toured England, headed the West Indies bowling table and been chosen as one of *Wisden*'s Cricketers of the Year – there were no official complaints about his bowling action on that tour. In 1966, however, he was nothing like as successful and in trying to recapture his earlier venom in some instances, flexed his arm to give the delivery extra pace. This resulted in his being no-balled by Arthur Fagg when the tourists met Lancashire at Old Trafford.

The epidemic of throwing was by now finished. Occasionally bowlers have transgressed the Law since 1966, but in the 18 years since then less than a dozen have been called. The following note was added to the Law concerning no-balling of a bowler due to throwing in 1967:

> A ball shall be deemed to have been thrown if, in the opinion of either umpire, the process of straightening the bowling arm, whether it be partial or complete, takes place during that part of the delivery swing which directly precedes the ball leaving the hand.

This note was retained when the Laws were completely redrafted in 1980.

7 D'Oliveira and After

In 1968 what became known as 'the D'Oliveira Affair' split English cricket opinion and brought to a head the question of the attitude the cricket world should take towards South Africa and its policy of *apartheid*.

Basil d'Oliveira was born in Signal Hill, Cape Town, in 1931. After great success in local club cricket, he was forced, being a Cape Coloured, to emigrate to England to seek higher levels of the game. John Arlott, the commentator and writer, helped him to a position in the Central Lancashire League with Middleton. After five years he qualified for Worcestershire, and the following year, 1966, he played for England. He was a forcing and skilful middle-order batsman, and a useful swing bowler. He was also a good competitor, whose best innings normally came when most wanted and whose wickets often broke dangerous partnerships.

From the time of his first selection for England, it was plain that there might be some conflict if ever he were chosen to tour South Africa, where under his country's policies, he was a second-class citizen. The possibility of such selection loomed in 1968.

In 1966 the New Zealand Rugby Board were refused permission to include Maoris in a side to tour South Africa, and cancelled the tour. The MCC, having toured South Africa the year before, were in New Zealand at the time, and the manager of the side, S. C. Griffith, was the MCC secretary. He went on record as agreeing with the rugby tour cancellation, implying that the MCC would make the same decision in similar circumstances. Later Griffith visited South Africa to meet the South African Cricket Association, and discussed the possibility of a

114

player of non-European descent in a visiting MCC side, but no conclusion was reached.

A statement in 1967 by the South African Minister of the Interior implied that d'Oliveira would not be acceptable as a tourist, prompting a statement in the House of Commons by Denis Howell, Minister for Sport, that MCC had told the Government that their teams would be chosen on merit, and no tour would be undertaken should any player be rejected by the host country.

Mr Vorster, the South African Prime Minister, himself made a statement in the House of Assembly, which confirmed that the country's policy of non-mixed sport would not be compromised, even for the best players, and that no negotiations were possible. MCC thus sought clarification in writing from the SACA in January 1968, and Sir Alec Douglas-Home, himself an MCC tourist to South America in 1926 and the previous year's MCC president, separately discussed the matter with Mr Vorster. No clear answer came from either, but on Sir Alec's advice plans for the 1968–69 tour went ahead.

D'Oliveira, meanwhile, had had mixed fortunes for England, but on the eve of the selection of the touring party was brought into the fifth Test against Australia at the Oval, when R. M. Prideaux was forced to withdraw. D'Oliveira scored a brilliant 158, and helped England to win and thereby draw the series.

When the touring party was announced immediately afterwards, there was consternation among the majority of cricket followers at the absence of d'Oliveira's name. It was widely assumed that the MCC, or the selectors (D. J. Insole, A. V. Bedser, P. B. H. May and D. Kenyon) had omitted him for political reasons, so as not to prejudice the tour. The selectors justified their choice, the chairman, Insole, explaining that d'Oliveira had been considered solely as a batsman and that others were thought more likely to succeed on South African wickets.

There were many, including knowledgeable players, who found this hard to accept, and a group of MCC members, led by the Rev D. S. Sheppard, a former England player, insisted on a special meeting to discuss the matter. A Sunday newspaper, the *News of the World*, meanwhile engaged d'Oliveira to report the forthcoming tour.

On 16 September, T. H. Cartwright, one of the selected tourists, was forced to withdraw, and the selectors announced that d'Oliveira would take his place. Cartwright could be regarded as an all-rounder, like d'Oliveira, but was principally a bowler who could bat usefully. D'Oliveira's supporters were not slow to point out that his substitution for Cartwright was not consistent with the selectors' reason for omitting him in the first place.

This fact was not lost on Mr Vorster, whose immediate reaction was that South Africa would not receive a team chosen for political purposes. A week later the MCC formally cancelled the tour. It should be said that d'Oliveira at the time remained discreet and dignified, and did not lose, then or since, any of the respect or popularity he enjoyed among the cricket public, irrespective of their views on the South African situation.

The special MCC meeting was held in December, with the Rev D. S. Sheppard and J. M. Brearley, later to captain England, speaking for the following resolutions:

1. That the Members of MCC regret their Committee's mishandling of affairs leading up to the selection of the team for the intended tour of South Africa in 1968–69.
2. That no further tours to or from South Africa be undertaken until credence can be given of actual progress by South Africa towards non-racial cricket.
3. That a Special Committee be set up to examine such proposals by the SACA towards non-racial cricket; the MCC to report on progress to the Annual General Meeting of the Club; and to the Governing Body for Cricket – the MCC Council.

The main cause for complaint against the MCC centred on their omission to extract from the SACA in advance a guarantee that any team selected would be accepted. This would have saved later embarrassment to d'Oliveira and argument among the members and selectors. The Committee's defence, mainly put by D. R. W. Silk and A. M. Crawley, was that they accepted Sir Alec Douglas-Home's advice that it would be impolitic to insist on an answer to hypothetical questions, and implied that South Africa's domestic policies were not the MCC's concern. It was also necessary to encourage cricket in all circumstances. M. C. Cowdrey, who would have captained the tourists and was therefore involved in selection, stated that the side was picked on merit.

All three resolutions were lost, both at the meeting and in the accompanying postal vote. The overall voting was 4357–1570, 4664–1214 and 4508–1352.

Those who lost the debate were nevertheless satisfied that the subject had been aired and the whole question of South African sporting links was thereafter seldom out of the news.

The South Africans were due to tour England in 1970, but first a rugby tour was scheduled for the winter of 1969–70. This caused bitter controversy, demonstrations, huge policing and security costs and even physical confrontations. Members of the police and public were injured during demonstrations, games were interrupted and many arrests were made.

A man who came into prominence as a spokesman against both the rugby and cricket tours was a young white South African studying in London, Peter Hain. In September 1969 he organized a Stop the Seventy Tour Committee, which advocated non-violent protest, and which rapidly gained support.

Denis Howell, in October, stated that the tourists should stay away, while Jack Cheetham, President of SACA, confirmed that the tour was on. S. C. Griffith, with the MCC vote behind him, repeated that the Cricket Council preferred the policy of 'building bridges' with South Africa to cutting links.

In December, the TCCB announced:

> The Test and County Cricket Board, comprising representatives from all first-class counties and the minor counties, have confirmed unanimously their recommendation that the South African tour will take place.
>
> In re-affirming this decision, they repeat their aversion to racial discrimination of any kind. They also respect the rights of those who wish to demonstrate peacefully.

The SACA stated that the South African party would be selected on merit, with no colour considerations; the South African

Cricket Board of Control, representing non-white cricket, described the statement as meaningless.

Anti-tour propaganda increased. David Sheppard, now Bishop of Woolwich, warned against violence, which would be counter-productive. Many Labour MPs and trade unionists announced their intentions to demonstrate. County clubs were asked by the Cricket Council to plan security arrangements for the tour.

In view of the growing concern, a meeting was held at the Home Office, between the MCC, James Callaghan, the Home Secretary, and Denis Howell, after which the Cricket Council announced a shortened tour, the original programme being roughly halved to 12 matches at the more 'secure' venues. The Prime Minister, Harold Wilson, accused the MCC of making a big mistake in proceeding with the tour.

On 23 April 1970, with the tourists' arrival only weeks away, a 1970 Cricket Fund was launched at Lord's with distinguished patrons. A Fair Cricket Campaign, with equally distinguished leaders, was also begun, with the object of stopping the tour, or, if unsuccessful, of organizing a huge peaceful protest at Lord's during the Test match. April also saw a major turn in events when the Supreme Council for Sport in Africa threatened the withdrawal of African countries from the Commonwealth Games in Edinburgh should the tour take place.

On 14 May, at the insistence of Philip Noel-Baker, an Olympic Games medalist, an emergency debate took place in the House of Commons, where Denis Howell identified four areas of public concern regarding the tour: the effects on racial harmony, law and order, the Commonwealth Games and the long-term interests of sport. He announced a resolution of the Sports Council urging the Cricket Council to withdraw the South Africans' invitation.

Then the International Olympic Committee took a hand. This body had been forced to reverse a decision to invite South Africa to the 1968 Olympics in the face of a threatened withdrawal by over 40 countries to boycott the Games. In May 1970 the SCSA, which had already threatened the Commonwealth Games over the tour, was instrumental in persuading the IOC to expel South Africa from the Olympic movement altogether.

Support for the cancellation of the tour was now widespread among many diverse sections of the community. Four days after the Commons debate, the Cricket Council met in secret. Afterwards, S. C. Griffith issued the following statement:

At a meeting held yesterday the Cricket Council – representing all grades of cricket in the United Kingdom -- were given a full report by the Executive Committee on all matters relating to the South African tour which had arisen since the Council's last meeting on April 23. The Council weighed carefully the strength of opinion both for and against the tour. This full statement of the Council's deliberations is indicative of their concern and of their awareness of the responsibilities with which they were faced.

The Council have decided by a substantial majority, that this tour should proceed as arranged. It has always believed that cricket in South Africa should be given the longest possible time to bring about conditions in which all cricketers in their own country, regardless of their origin, are able to play and be selected on equal terms. The South African Cricket Association have taken the first step by announcing that all future touring teams will be selected on merit. The Council have confirmed the present tour in the hope and belief that this intention will be capable of fulfilment in the future. It is for this reason that the Council, while confirming finally their invitation to the South African Cricket Association to tour this summer, wish to make clear their position regarding the future.

They have informed the South African Cricket Association that no further Test tours between South African and this country will take place until South African cricket is played and teams are selected on a multi-racial basis in South Africa.

In this increasingly complicated issue the Council felt that they should first reassess their responsibilities. These they confirmed as being contained in the following broad headings:

1. To cricket and cricketers both in the United Kingdom and throughout the world:
2. To other sports and sportsmen.

It should be stressed that the Council have taken into account other matters of a public and political nature, but they consider those matters to be the responsibility of the Government who are best equipped to judge and act upon them.

In reviewing their original decision to confirm the invitation to the South African Cricket Association, the Council had to consider whether the desirability – so often repeated – of maintaining contact with South Africa had in any way changed. It was agreed that in the long term this policy was in the best interests of cricket, and cricketers of all races in South Africa. The Council had also to consider its responsibilities to cricket and cricketers throughout the world, taking into account the opposition to the tour from certain quarters and the effect on other cricket-playing countries if the tour proceeded. The Council sympathised with those Boards of Control who had themselves been put under considerable pressure in regard to this tour but felt that the long term effects upon cricket could be disastrous if they were to succumb to similar pressure.

The Council also had to consider whether cricket would be a practical proposition if played amidst all the stresses and strains which have been threatened and predicted. The Council were under no illusions as to the risks of disruption at the matches to be played. They had also to consider the recent statement of the Home Secretary in the House of Commons on May 14 that 'there need be no fear in anybody's mind that the police are incapable of handling this kind of demonstration'. They also noted his assurance that it would be the duty of the police to prevent a breach of the peace and bring them (the offenders) before the courts.

The Council discussed the question of the Commonwealth Games in Scotland and deeply regretted the attitude of those countries who had threatened to withdraw if the cricket tour took place. The Council acknowledged a degree of responsibility to other sports and recognised the problems with which the organising bodies are faced. They hope, in view of their statement as to the future, that these countries will reconsider their attitude.

Two other issues which have already been mentioned should perhaps be further elaborated.

First, the question of community relations. The Council recognise that there has been a growing concern in the United Kingdom with the unacceptable apartheid policies of the present South African Government. The Council share this concern, but wish to re-emphasise that cricket has made an outstanding and widely acknowledged contribution to the maintenance of good relations between all people among whom the game has been played.

Secondly, the question of freedom under the law in this country. The Council do not consider it the duty or responsibility of cricket to campaign for freedom under the law at the expense of the game itself. But the Council and its constituent members are aware of the dangers of a minority group being allowed to take the law into their own hands by direct action. However distasteful to this minority group, the South African tour this summer is not only a lawful event, but as shown by the outcome of recent opinion polls, it is clearly the wish of the majority that the tour should take place.

The Cricket Council, by this statement, seemed to abandon common sense for the luxury of sticking to a principle. The 'responsibility to other sports' had been acknowledged, but had not apparently carried much weight. Opposition to the tour increased in size and intensity. It was becoming clear that a peaceful and satisfactory test of the cricketing skill of the two countries would be impossible. South African opinion, faced with a rapidly growing isolation from international sport, was desperate for the tour to proceed, despite growing awareness that considering the scale of the protest in England, any ill-judged gesture or accidental incident could lead to physical danger.

In this atmosphere, James Callaghan invited the Chairman and Secretary of the Cricket Council to the Home Office and later sent this letter to the Chairman, M. J. C. Allom:

When you and Mr Griffith came to see me this morning, we discussed the statement issued on behalf of the Cricket Council on May 19 about the South African tour.

You explained that the Council had come to their conclusion that the tour should go on after reassessing their own responsibilities, which were limited to the impact of the decision on cricket and cricketers, both in the United Kingdom and throughout the world, and on other sports and sportsmen. You emphasized however that although the Council were naturally concerned with various other matters of a public and political nature which had been brought to their notice and had taken them into account, at the same time they felt that these matters fell outside their own responsibilities and that it was beyond their competence to judge what significance to attach to them. This, they felt, was the responsibility of the Government, who were equipped to judge and act upon them. I accept this distinction.

The Government have therefore been very carefully considering the implications of the tour, if it were to take place, in the light of the many representations that have been received from a wide variety of interests and persons. We have had particularly in mind the possible impact on relations with other Commonwealth countries, race relations with other Commonwealth countries, race relations in this country and the divisive effect on the community. Another matter for concern is the effect on the Commonwealth Games. I have taken into account too the position of the police; there is no doubt as to their ability to cope with any situation which might arise, but a tour of this nature would mean diverting police resources on a large scale from their essential ordinary duties.

The Government have come to the conclusion, after reviewing all these considerations, that on grounds of broad public policy they must request the Cricket Council to withdraw their invitation to the South African Cricket Association, and I should be grateful if you would put this request before the Council.

The next day, 22 May, only nine days before the South Africans were due to arrive, the Cricket Council issued the following statement:

At a meeting held this afternoon at Lord's, the Cricket

Council considered the formal request from Her Majesty's Government to withdraw the invitation to the South African touring team this summer.

With deep regret the Council were of the opinion that they had no alternative but to accede to this request and they are informing the South African Cricket Association accordingly. The Council are grateful for the overwhelming support of cricketers, cricket lovers and may others, and share their disappointment at the cancellation of the tour. At the same time they regret the discourtesy to the South African Cricket Association and the inconvenience caused to so many people.

The Council see no reason to repeat the arguments to which they still adhere which led them to sustain the invitation to the South African cricketers issued four years ago. They do, however, deplore the activities of those who by the intimidation of individual cricketers and threats of violent disruption have inflamed the whole issue.

Thus 80 years of cricket between England and South Africa came to an end.

The influence of the other African countries on the position of South Africa in international sports continued. The policies of the management of the game of rugby union have often led to contention. Despite the rebuff over its selection of Maoris in 1966, New Zealand sent a team to South Africa in 1976. African nations threatened to withdraw from the Olympic Games if New Zealand were not barred. New Zealand took part, and 22 African nations withdrew.

No doubt to prevent a similar withdrawal from the Commonwealth Games of 1978, Commonwealth heads of government drew up in 1977 at Gleneagles a declaration headed 'Apartheid in Sport'. This was intended to unite Commonwealth countries in a policy which would preclude international competition with South Africa until that country allowed multi-racial sport from club level upwards and selection on merit. However it suffers from lack of precise definitions and is now liable to be cited by opposing shades of opinion. The legislators of rugby union, which is, in theory at least, an amateur game, tend to ignore it where possible.

In 1981 an England team was chosen to tour India and Sri Lanka. Included were G. Boycott and G. Cook, players who had recently appeared in South African cricket. It was announced from India that these players would not be acceptable in India, and the tour was within an ace of being cancelled. It took the intervention of Prime Minister Mrs Gandhi and statements from Boycott and Cook condemning *apartheid* before the tour was allowed to proceed, less than a week before departure time.

Soon after the return of the England party, it was announced that 12 English cricketers had agreed to play a series, including three 'Test' matches, in South Africa. Boycott was among the 12, and thought to be one of the recruiting agents. Other Test players in the squad were D. L. Amiss, J. E. Emburey, G. A. Gooch, M. Hendrick, A. P. E. Knott, W. Larkins, J. K. Lever, C. M. Old, D. L. Underwood and P. Willey, while R. A. Woolmer was one of two additions to the party. The tour was organized by the South African Cricket Union, formed in 1977 by the merging of the 'white' SACA and the 'black' SACBOC, although dissidents from the SACBOC had immediately formed the South African Cricket Board, leaving two opposing bodies as before. The team was known as the South African Breweries England XI, after the sponsors.

The same season a team from Sri Lanka, which had only weeks before played its first Test match, toured South Africa. The TCCB had to act in respect of the English cricketers to protect the following summer's tours by India and Pakistan and met on 19 March when the following rule was adopted:

> The cricketers who have formed a team to play representative matches against representative teams in South Africa in March 1982 will be ineligible for selection for England for a period of three years from 15 April 1982 and the same ineligibility shall apply to any other cricketers joining any part of the tour being undertaken by that team.

The Sri Lankans, who were not of the same calibre as cricketers, were banned from first-class cricket for 25 years.

Meanwhile, conflict was growing in the West Indies. As early as 1959 a tour to South Africa to be led by F. M. Worrell was cancelled because of controversy. The tour had been arranged with the SACBOC, and three 'Tests', in addition to other matches, were scheduled against non-white opponents. The tour was cancelled because the view prevailed that it tacitly accepted *apartheid*. There had been minor incidents concerning links with South Africa during the 1970s. In 1970, G. St. A. Sobers, the West Indies captain, was refused entry into Guyana until he apologised for a trip to Rhodesia. In 1974 a team organized by D. H. Robins was not allowed in Guyana or Trinidad and Tobago because Robins also took sides to South Africa – the tour was confined to the Leeward Islands and Barbados. In 1976 an England Youth team was refused entry to Guyana and Jamaica because members had played in South Africa. There was internal strife also in 1976, when Guyana refused to admit G. A. Greenidge of Barbados because he had toured South Africa, and the Shell Shield match was consequently cancelled.

The first major international incident occurred in 1981, also in Guyana. The England touring party was due to play the second Test in Georgetown, commencing 28 February. The England fast bowler, R. G. D. Willis, had broken down and R. D. Jackman arrived as replacement. Two days before the Test was due to start, the Guyana government expelled Jackman, on the grounds that he had played cricket in South Africa. The English authorities refused to play the Test and the party flew to Barbados as the West Indian governments took stock of the situation. Eventually it was decided that the tour should proceed thenceforth as arranged. This remains the only Test match to be cancelled days before its scheduled start for political reasons.

In 1981–82, the Guyana batsman, A. I. Kallicharran, who had not been chosen for a tour of Australia, played for Transvaal, and was thus banned for life by the West Indies Cricket Board of Control under a policy adopted in 1976. Tempting offers to play in South Africa were extended to C. H. Lloyd, the West Indian captain, and I. V. A. Richards, perhaps the world's leading batsman, and although declined, made the authorities apprehensive. But few could have expected the events of January 1983.

On 4 January the West Indies was shocked by news of a proposed South African tour by a team containing several established West Indian players, including current Test players. At least 18 players were named in various reports, and Sir Garfield Sobers was listed as manager. There were many immediate denials including one from Sobers. It seemed the proposed tour was cancelled.

On 10 January, however, it was discovered that several players were booked to fly to Miami next morning, *en route* for South Africa. Among them were L. G. Rowe and C. E. H. Croft, who had been congratulated publicly four days earlier by A. F. Rae, President of the WICBC, for rejecting the South African offers.

The full team in South Africa was L. G. Rowe, R. A. Austin, E. H. Mattis, H. S. Chang, R. R. Wynter (all from Jamaica); A. E. Greenidge, S. T. Clarke, F. daC. Stephenson, E. A. Moseley, E. T. Trotman, C. L. King, D. A. Murray (all Barbados); D. R. Parry (Leeward Islands); C. E. H. Croft, A. I. Kallicharran (Guyana); and B. D. Julien (Trinidad and Tobago). These players were not crucial to any future West Indian Test team, and there was relief when among those who declined contracts at the last minute were the Test batsman D. L. Haynes and fast bowler M. D. Marshall.

This was the first West Indian team of any kind to tour South Africa, and discussion of the merit of the tour was fierce in the West Indies for several weeks. While cricket authorities and the media condemned the players, public opinion was surprisingly tolerant. Some of the players were out of work, and were not criticised harshly for accepting US$100 000 for two seasons' work. They had left on the tour surreptitiously, but found on their return that they could even wear their South African blazers with impunity.

The tour was a major success from South Africa's point of view. Two 'Tests' were played on the famous grounds of Newlands in Cape Town and the Wanderers in Johannesburg. South African cricket, which the results suggested had declined during its lack of international competition, was given a big stimulus.

In November 1983 the second West Indian party arrived in South Africa. Austin, Chang and Wynter had been paid off, and replaced by stronger players, H. L. Alleyne (Barbados), S. F. A. Bacchus and M. A. Lynch (both Guyana). The situation of

Lynch caused discussion in England, where he played for Surrey and was qualified to play for England. The TCCB ruled that his inclusion in the party meant that he forfeited his English status, but on legal advice this decision was later rescinded.

This tour was not at first sponsored, companies being worried about action by the newly legal black trade unions. All three previous tours had lost money. However it was suspected, although denied, that Government funds had always been available for such enterprises.

There was bad feeling when it transpired that the West Indians were attempting to set up a private sponsorship deal. The President of SACU, Joe Pamensky, reacted with bitterness, and the tourists threatened not to play in the next fixture, but were content merely to refuse the maroon flannels in favour of white. Ill-feeling was apparent on the field, however. Eventually sponsorship for the remainder of the tour appeared.

A well-publicized incident early in the tour concerned Colin Croft, who attempted to travel to the Newlands ground by train, and was ordered out of a whites-only compartment, providing propaganda for the anti-tour supporters, and giving the tourists a rare glimpse of *apartheid* realities.

The dilemma that faces world cricket in 1984 in deciding how to treat South Africa lies in the difficulty of finding a course of action to benefit both cricket and those oppressed by South African government policy, which most agree is abhorrent.

Those who want to play with South Africa assert that to influence that policy it is necessary to maintain contact. It is also said that South African cricket has gone at least as far as anybody could expect in providing multi-racial cricket. The South African Cricket Union, by merging in 1977 three existing national bodies, the South African Cricket Board, the South African Cricket Association and the South African Cricket Board of Control, officially united for the first time South African cricketers of all races on equal terms. It is alleged that in not re-admitting South Africa into the Test fold, the ICC has not honoured an obligation to do so when racial barriers were lowered.

Those who do not want to play with South Africa claim that some sort of protest is necessary, and that non-white opinion in South Africa supports the ban. The SACU might have merged existing authorities, but it could not unify opinion, as was shown by the formation of a new body, the South African Cricket Board, allied to the South African Council on Sport and backed by the Supreme Council for Sports in Africa, all of whom support sporting isolation for South Africa. Two protesters greeted the West Indian rebel tourists in 1983, one carrying a banner which said 'Freedom first, cricket later', the majority non-white view. The SACU's moves towards multi-racialism are seen as cosmetic – manoeuvres to attract international competition. That no real dent in *apartheid* in other walks of life is apparent only makes these moves more distasteful.

While official tours are barred, there is the equally complex question of how to treat those who go on private tours.

In 1983 an English women's tour to the West Indies was cancelled four days before the party was due to leave because the Caribbean Women's Cricket Federation banned five members of the party who had played in South Africa four years previously. When the West Indies rebel tour was announced, the Australian Prime Minister, Malcolm Frazer, banned the tourists from entering that country, including D. A. Murray, whose wife is Australian and at the time was expecting a baby in Australia.

In some way or another, players who have toured South Africa privately have suffered bans. Many hold that this is unjust, and encroaches on individual freedom. The point has been made that the TCCB condoned the tours that D. H. Robins made to South Africa in the 1970s, when there was no attempt at multi-racial cricket, but condemned the players who went in 1982, when there was. There are many, too, who think that players should be allowed to earn where they can. Britain's trade with South Africa amounts to nearly £2000 million per year. If thousands of companies and shareholders can sell goods and services to South Africa, why condemn cricketers who sell their talents? Similar arguments were used when attempts were made to discourage athletes from attending the 1980 Moscow Olympics – why should sportsmen suffer when business proceeds as usual? If the Moscow argument is sound, the South African one is, too.

There is considerable hypocrisy in the dealings with players.

At the time of the West Indian rebel tour, the government of Barbados, the home of several of the rebels, was noticeably less keen on imposing punishments than other West Indian authorities. Barbados had just banned British jockeys from riding there because they had ridden in South Africa. However, Louis Tull, Barbados Minister of Foreign Affairs, was clear in stating there was no question of penalising the cricketers. Bans are less attractive when they penalise the home team.

What of the future? There were rumours during the 1983 World Cup of impending coups for the South African Cricket Union. It was published later in South Africa that seven leading Australians had signed to play there. Naturally, all stories are denied. But South Africa is a rich country, and wants international cricket. Other tours will take place.

There are persistent moves for MCC to send a team to South Africa. The latest was defeated in July 1983, a poll of MCC members voting 6604 to 4344 against it. The 40 per cent in favour no doubt encouraged the SACU.

The 'problem' of South Africa will disappear only when *apartheid* is abolished, and there is no sign of this. Meanwhile the problem cannot be solved, as it contains so many interwoven and conflicting strands.

8 The Kerry Packer Affair

When Sir Frank Packer, an Australian newspaper and television tycoon, died in 1974, his younger son, Kerry, took over the empire. Within three years Kerry Packer had loosened the roots of a game which had spread its branches around the world.

Packer had long been interested in sports and from the start of his chairmanship of Channel 9, one of Australia's five television stations, had been anxious to promote cricket and make use of its appeal to television audiences. In fact, one of his first discussions with his executives had floated the idea of an independent cricket series. His main objective, however, was to televise Test cricket, which was due for its centenary in 1977. Packer approached the Australian Cricket Board with a proposal by which he would televise matches played under its auspices. Packer wanted exclusive rights, for which he was prepared to pay substantially. From a business point of view it was an offer which the Australian Board would find difficult to decline.

However, the Board did decline. They were against the granting of exclusive rights on principle, and in addition they had always dealt with the state-owned Australian Broadcasting Commission and were reluctant to change.

Kerry Packer was angry at this rebuff. His offer had been a good one (it is said he invited the Board to name its own price) and he felt that 'establishment' interests were combining against him. In his frustration he devised the scheme which blossomed into World Series Cricket.

The plan was to sign on private contracts as many as possible of the world's leading players to enable a series of matches to be played outside the jurisdiction of the Australian Board. The matches and players would be marketed and exploited by

Packer companies and their associates, and, of course, would be televised exclusively on Channel 9.

The problems were to make the plans, to discuss them with players from various countries and to sign contracts with them, while keeping the activity secret all the while from the cricketing authorities who, it was rightly suspected, would do all they could to prevent the operation.

The advantage Packer had was that the time was ripe for such a coup. For years cricketers had been complaining gently about low pay and poor conditions. In 1968 a Cricketers' Association had been formed in English cricket with the purpose of improving the status of the professional cricketer, and to provide cricketers with a voice in the development of the game. It was a weak voice at first, as many players regarded it with apathy, but by 1977, with John Arlott as President, it had achieved a near 100 per cent membership. Judged as a trade union it is moderate, and its role in the Packer affair, as will be seen later, was based on compromise, with the well-being of both its members and the game as a whole as its concern.

In Australia, the situation was more complex. Less cricket is played, and Australian cricketers were obliged to have jobs outside the game. Their rewards directly from cricket were comparatively small. However, in the 1976–77 season, the Cricket Board had instituted a sub-committee, which included the State captains, with the aim of giving the players more influence in the organization of the game, particularly in the financial rewards to be obtained from sponsorship. This coincided with improvements in the players' payment for Test matches, the basic fee having double in two years with sizeable bonuses being paid. Greg Chappell, the Australian captain, wrote in a book just prior to the Centenary Test that 'Australia leads the way in providing a far better deal for cricketers.'

However, sports sponsorship was booming in the 1970s. Sports agencies had made millionaires of sportsmen like golfer Jack Nicklaus (a friend of Kerry Packer) and tennis player Bjorn Borg. On the scale relating fame to wealth, cricketers were near the bottom.

Many of Australia's leading sportsmen, including Dennis Lillee, were associated with an agency called J. P. Sport. Soon after Kerry Packer had been 'snubbed' by the Australian Cricket Board, a meeting took place between J. P. Sport and Packer's Television Corporation Ltd. Between them they formulated the package of World Series Cricket and began to approach the players. They were helped by the Centenary Test match taking place in Melbourne on 12–17 March 1977, when many of the players they wished to sign were together in one place.

The initial success of the enterprise was astonishing, both in the readiness of leading players to sign contracts, and in the secrecy which was maintained despite the presence in force at the Centenary Test of the world's cricketing journalists.

The first hint that something out of the ordinary was afoot was contained in a report in South Africa's *Sunday Times* on 24 April 1977 which stated that four South African cricketers had signed contracts to play in a series of matches throughout the world. The significance of this report was overlooked by the world at large, no doubt because since South Africa had been outlawed from Test cricket, many of the leading players were already playing as 'mercenaries' in other parts of the world.

The news which really rocked the world of cricket came on 9 May and was contained in *The Bulletin*, a magazine in the Kerry Packer empire. It was announced that 35 cricketers had signed a three-year deal with J. P. Sports and Television Corporation Ltd., by which they would play a series of specially arranged matches, beginning in Australia in 1977–78.

The 35 players comprised an impressive list. Eighteen were Australian: I. M. Chappell, R. J. Bright, G. S. Chappell, I. C. Davis, R. Edwards, G. J. Gilmour, D. W. Hookes, D. K. Lillee, M. F. Malone, R. W. Marsh, R. B. McCosker, K. J. O'Keeffe, L. S. Pascoe, I. R. Redpath, R. D. Robinson, J. R. Thomson, M. H. N. Walker and K. D. Walters. Five came from South Africa: E. J. Barlow, D. L. Hobson, R. G. Pollock, M. J. Procter and B. A. Richards. Four were from England: A. W. Greig, A. P. E. Knott, J. A. Snow and D. L. Underwood. Four were West Indian: M. A. Holding, C. H. Lloyd, I. V. A. Richards and A. M. E. Roberts. The remaining four were from Pakistan: Asif Iqbal, Imran Khan, Majid Khan and Mushtaq Mohammad.

By this time the Australian touring party had arrived in

England for the 1977 season. There was a strong resemblance between the party and the Packer squad. The notable absentees were Lillee (who was recovering from an injury) and Ian Chappell (who had retired, but returned for the Packer bonanza). The manager, Len Maddocks, was quoted as saying that he did not envisage the tour being affected by the Packer revelations, but that if any of the cricketers played for a side contrary to the jurisdiction of the Australian Board, they would place their careers in jeopardy. The first reaction of the Test and County Cricket Board was that the problem appeared to be one mainly for Australia, but the following day they announced that they would be meeting the English players involved as soon as possible.

Meanwhile it was reported in Australia that the Brisbane curator, or groundsman, had resigned to join Mr Packer, and that Mr Packer was hoping to persuade the Australian authorities to alter the dates fixed for the 1977–78 Indian tour of Australia to fit in with his own arrangements. Greg Chappell and Tony Greig were appointed captains of Packer's 'Australia' and 'The Rest of the World'. Berkeley Gaskin, President of the Guyana Cricket Board, stated that the West Indian players would need approval from their own Board of Control before they could play for Kerry Packer.

It rapidly became clear that the England captain, Tony Greig, had played an important part in the recruitment of players for the Kerry Packer 'circus', as it was beginning to be called. Indeed, he had been Packer's chosen lieutenant to advocate the scheme to the overseas players. In an interview Greig confirmed he would play for Packer, even if it meant resigning the England captaincy. He stated that he had declined to ask advice from Lord's while negotiations were progressing because he knew what the answer would be. He continued by announcing the arrangements for the Packer season: 54 days of cricket including six five-day 'Tests', six one-day games and six three-day round-robin tournaments.

Geoffrey Boycott emerged as the most prominent cricketer to refuse the terms offered by Kerry Packer. It appeared he was prepared to play a series in Australia, but would not accept a contract mentioning a later series in England, as that would conflict with his Yorkshire contract.

Ghulam Ahmed, the secretary of the Indian Cricket Board, stated that he had been in touch with the Australian Board about the forthcoming official tour and gave his opinion that Mr Packer's project would ruin world cricket.

On Friday, 11 May, two days after the Packer series had been announced, the Cricket Council held an emergency meeting at Lord's. The meeting concluded that until a meeting of the International Cricket Conference could be held and the situation reviewed, the English players who had signed for Packer would be selected on merit for the summer's Tests. However, Alec Bedser, the chairman of the selectors, was instructed not to consider Tony Greig when selecting the captain, on the grounds that Greig had recruited players for a series of cricket matches which would conflict with those officially arranged and he had not sought the advice of the Council before doing so. He had impaired the trust existing between the authorities and the England captain. 'The captaincy of the England team', said F. R. Brown, Chairman of the Council, 'involves close liaison with the selectors in the management, selection and development of England players for the future and clearly Greig is unlikely to be able to do this as his stated intention is to be contracted elsewhere during the next three winters'.

Greig was not surprised to lose the England captaincy. It is probable that when he decided to act for Kerry Packer he realised his life was changing direction towards Australia. He was courteous and plausible when explaining the reasons for his actions and claimed that cricketers in general would benefit, a claim that bears examination in the light of events. However, of all the characters involved in the saga of World Series Cricket, he was the most bitterly attacked in the press, and remains the man the 'traditionalists' find it hardest to forgive. His record as England captain was good, and during the 1976–77 tour of India, his last series as captain, England had already begun to play with the spirit and urgency which his successor, Mike Brearley, who admirably maintained the momentum, is usually given sole credit for. Greig's talent disappeared overnight in the eyes of the English press and even his South African birth was suddenly held against him.

So far as the Australians were concerned the Cricket Board was not only bitter in their attitude towards Kerry Packer, but, like the Cricket Council in its attitude to Greig, felt betrayed by many of the players who had signed for the rebel 'circus.' The cricket sub-committee had met just two days before the Centenary Test, and discussed the revenue arising from a new Benson and Hedges sponsorship. Four of the State captains on that sub-committee, formed on the understanding that the Board would remain the only promoter of matches against teams from overseas, had nevertheless signed contracts for Mr Packer, whose intention was to promote matches in rivalry. The Board were as surprised by the announcement of 9 May as the English authorities.

However, with the Australian tourists already in England, with Greg Chappell as captain, the Board had either to accept the situation for the rest of the English summer or to cancel the remainder of the tour. Had the Cricket Council instructed the England selectors to ignore the Packer men, the Australian Board would have been under pressure to recall the tourists, but both authorities opted to mark time for the present.

Kerry Packer was anxious to reach a working agreement with 'official' cricket. He came to England and at a Press conference claimed that his series was not so much a 'pirate' venture as a series of 'Super-Tests'. He expressed a willingness to compromise, but claimed the cricketing bodies were not replying to his telegrams.

On 14 June, at an emergency meeting of the International Cricket Conference, it was agreed to discuss his plans with Mr Packer as soon as possible. Talks were arranged for 23 June, when Packer would be back from a visit to the United States.

With Mr Packer at those talks were three colleagues, David McNicoll, Lynton Taylor and Richie Benaud. Richie Benaud had been one of Australia's most successful captains in the 1960s and had since become one of the best and most respected commentators on the game. His company had been engaged as public relations consultants to World Series Cricket, and Benaud was to be a valuable adviser to Packer on the conduct of the matches.

The ICC were prepared to come to terms with Kerry Packer provided he could satisfy them on various counts: the Packer series should not exceed six weeks, should obey the laws of cricket and should be under the auspices of the home authority, who would need to approve the programme and venues and to grant permission to take part to the players, whose availability for Tests and other 'official' games would take precedence. Also, the home authority would require to be able to honour existing contractual arrangements with sponsors and advertisers, and none of Mr Packer's teams should be represented as the national team.

The discussions proceeded well, but foundered on one condition of Mr Packer: that Channel 9 be granted exclusive television rights to cricket by the Australian Board as soon as the existing contract with the Australian Broadcasting Commission ended.

The Australian Board refused to accept this condition, arguing again against the principle of exclusive rights, and when the ICC backed this view, the talks ended.

Mr Packer's line hardened, and in announcing his unwillingness to help the ruling bodies further, he stated that he now had 50 players under contract. It was known that D. L. Amiss of England, and four more West Indians, C. G. Greenidge, B. D. Julien, A. I. Kallicharran and C. L. King had signed contracts.

After this meeting, many observers whose first opinion of the proposed Packer circus was that it was merely a complicated and expensive ploy to force the Australian Board to accept his tender for television rights, now began to realise that it threatened the entire structure of cricket. Now that talks had broken down Mr Packer made it known that he would fight the authorities to prevent victimization of his players. It seemed that no longer was it possible for the Packer circus to be incorporated into the regular programme. The two factions were at war, and Mr Packer had most of the big guns. Should the split become complete, the world's best cricketers would be engaged on a razzmatazz jamboree, hyped up to attract less committed followers to watch television, while the traditional game, including Test matches, would be devalued.

The formal 'declaration of war' came at the ICC meeting at Lord's on 26 July. The mood was that the Packer circus should be outlawed and the players punished by being made ineligible for Test matches. The Packer 'exhibition' matches would not be regarded as first-class, would not appear in official cricket records, and would be 'disapproved'. But the resolution, passed unanimously, which finally split the Packer group from the rest of cricket read: 'No player who after 1 October 1977 has played or has made himself available to play in a match previously disapproved by the Conference shall thereafter be eligible to play in any Test match.'

The Australian agent for Jeff Thomson and Alvin Kallicharran, Mr David Lord, announced that these two players had withdrawn from the circus. Zaheer Abbas, of Pakistan, on the other hand, signed for Mr Packer.

Kerry Packer applied for an injunction and damages in the High Court against the ICC and the TCCB. A temporary injunction was granted against David Lord, whom Packer claimed had wrongfully induced his players to break their contracts with him.

The Test and County Cricket Board, meeting at Lord's on 10 August, confirmed a new sub-rule which in effect prevented Counties from playing for two years any cricketer who had made himself available for a Packer match. The implementation of these new rules, was, of course, subject to the decision of the High Court case to follow.

Meanwhile, R. A. Woolmer, of England, had joined the Packer circus, while the West Australia Cricket Association decided to ban its Packer players: Edwards, Lillee, Malone, Marsh and B. M. Laird.

The High Court hearing began on 26 September 1977 before Mr Justice Slade. The defendants were the ICC and the TCCB, and the plaintiffs, seeking to have the new rules declared void as a restraint of trade, were World Series Cricket Pty Ltd and three players, Tony Greig, John Snow and Mike Procter.

Mr Robert Alexander QC for the plaintiffs, said that for the first time cricketers were being given security of earnings during the winter – £12,000 as against £3,000 earned by those lucky enough to be selected for the previous winter's MCC tour. None of the players had contracts with their Counties during the winter, and all were free to sign for Packer. The bans were dictatorial and penal. Mr Packer had improved Test cricketers' earnings. The cricket earnings of the plaintiffs were stated to be under £10,000 per year for Greig, £7,500 for Procter and between £3,000 and £4,000 for Snow.

Tony Greig began his evidence on the third day. He stated the establishment needed a shake-up. Restrictions on wives accompanying tourists were unreasonable and £210 for a Test appearance totally inadequate. That it had already been increased to £1,000 was a direct result of Packer's challenge. Questioned by Mr Richard Kempster QC for the defendants, he asserted that winter opportunities for cricketers were limited and several were forced to go on the dole. He agreed benefits were welcome, but in evidence had stated that the sort of work involved in organizing them was degrading.

John Snow revealed that he had spent the winter of 1968–69 on the dole, and that he was convinced cricket would be best served by allowing the top players to play for Mr Packer's company.

Kerry Packer gave evidence on the fifth day. He said that if the ban held he would consider bringing his Super Tests to England. He liked cricket, and was involved in setting up coaching schools. He pointed out that Australian cricketers had responded to his offer with frightening alacrity, and that he was bringing back to the game players who had retired, including Ian Chappell, Dennis Lillee and Ian Redpath. Cross-questioned, he agreed he had ideas of using eight cameras and wiring bowlers for sound and that the viewer would more easily spot umpire's wrong decisions. He had little confidence in the Australian Cricket Board, which had accepted $A85,000 over three years for television rights from the Australian Broadcasting Company, rather than $A2.5 million over five years from his own company. He claimed the 'Super Tests' were good for cricket, television and the players. Only one player, Geoffrey Boycott, had refused to join him.

Alan Knott and Derek Underwood gave evidence on behalf

of Greig, Snow and Procter. Knott said he expected to earn £11,500 from cricket in 1977, and had been forced to sign on as unemployed when the 1968 tour to South Africa was cancelled. Underwood stated that he had spent one winter doing PR work for a company but entertaining customers had led him to put on 21 lb in weight and had been detrimental to his cricket. He said he was worried about his future after his retirement.

On the ninth day the ICC and TCCB were given leave to amend their defence under the 1974 Trade Union and Labour Relations Act, under which employer's associations cannot be sued for restraint of trade or inducement to break contracts.

Opening for the defence, Mr Michael Kempster said the authorities admitted some merits in Mr Packer's plans and regretted negotiations with him had broken down. He claimed that the concept of World Series was not philanthropic or a step to benefit cricketers but a calculated threat to the Australian Cricket Board. Mr Packer's series differed from other cricket in that it was administered by professionals to take money out of the game, and threatened the structure and viability of cricket all over the world.

In the third week of the case various officials gave evidence for the defence. Mr Raymond Steele, treasurer of the Australian Board, said Mr Packer's series would have a disastrous effect on conventional cricket. Mr Peter Short, a West Indian representative at the ICC, said the West Indians had reservations about a retroactive ban on Packer players, but had supported the ban to present a united front. He said the loss of players would make it difficult to produce a West Indies team and wondered if the withdrawal of sponsorship by Gillette from the West Indian Gillette Cup was due to the possible absence of the Packer players.

Geoffrey Boycott, on the sixteenth day (Monday, 17 October), revealed that he had had a phone call from Tony Greig at the weekend. Mr Justice Slade thought the remarks seemed of a jocular variety, but warned that he would take a serious view of attempts to influence witnesses. Boycott agreed that leading cricketers were badly paid, but said a man could not serve two masters, and felt that the absence of Packer players would considerably affect official Test matches.

Doug Insole, Chairman of the TCCB, said that the TCCB hoped there would be no need to ban anybody, that compromise could still be reached and that Mr Packer's series could be fitted into the first-class season. The action being recommended was only to be used in the extreme case. Should Mr Packer bring his cricketers to England, however, the authorities would do everything they could to prevent his enterprise succeeding. He confirmed that Mr Packer had offered the TCCB £150,000 for exclusive television rights of the 1977 England v Australia series, twice the asking price. Mr Insole stated that the ICC were willing to change the dates of some of the forthcoming Australia v India Tests and would offer Mr Packer the use of some cricket grounds and first-class status for his games in an attempt to avoid fixture clashes, but Mr Lynton Taylor, a senior Packer executive, stated that Mr Packer rejected the compromise plan.

After twelve witnesses had given evidence for the defendants, Mr Kempster began his closing address. He claimed that some contracts between players and World Series Cricket were in law void because they were unduly restrictive. A player would be paid only if selected for a match and if not selected any money paid in advance would be recoverable. If the contracts were in fact void, then allegations that the ICC and TCCB had induced players to break them failed.

The closing speech for the plaintiffs was made by Mr Andrew Morritt QC, who spoke for 12½ hours. He gave four reasons to reject the bans: they would inflict damage on seven of the next 13 Test tours; they were designed to preserve monopoly; the retroactive element was against public interest on fairness alone; and they deprived the public of the right to watch these cricketers.

The hearing ended in its seventh week, after 31 working days, or 137 hours. The judgment took 5½ hours to deliver.

Mr Justice Slade said two points had to be born in mind regarding the United Kingdom players: first, the neither the Cricket Council (recognised by the ICC as the governing body in England) nor the TCCB had been committed to offer them employment in the future, and second, that none of the players had contracts with the Cricket Council or TCCB which precluded them from playing for a private contractor.

His Lordship stated that the defendants firmly believed that the emergence of WSC and its threat to the ICC's promotion of first-class cricket was bad for the game. However, the question for the court was whether the actions taken by the ICC and TCCB to counter WSC were legally justified. His Lordship was satisfied that the benefits which might arise from the imposition of the bans on players who had signed for WSC were rather speculative.

The disadvantages of applying the bans were more apparent. They would remove from the players areas of livelihood and subject them to the injustice of retrospective legislation. They would deprive the public for some years of seeing the players in conventional cricket, which carried the risk that its appeal and profitability would be reduced. By imposing the bans, the defendants had not considered the contracts between WSC and the players, and these contracts were entitled to the protection of the law. Although the defendants had the best interests of cricket at heart as they saw them, that was not enough to justify in law the course they had taken.

Mr Justice Slade expressed surprise that a private sponsor had not challenged established cricket earlier. He also considered that the players could not be blamed for making their contracts in secret, although he understood the criticism of Greig, who was in a special position as Captain of England.

In his judgment be granted the players and WSC declarations that the rule changes of the ICC and TCCB banning the players from Test and County Cricket were *ultra vires* and void as being in unreasonable restraint of trade. The plaintiffs were awarded costs.

The decision, while it could have been expected, was a terrific blow to the cricket authorities, establishing some respectability for rivals which they had been inclined to regard with contempt. Individual counties regarded the verdict with differing views. Those whose teams contained a strong Packer element, such as Sussex, with Greig, Snow and Imran Khan, and Gloucestershire, with Procter and Zaheer Abbas, could be relieved that their stars would remain available to win matches and draw spectators.

Meanwhile the English season of 1977 had come to a close. The Australian tourists, from whom most of WSC's 'Australia' would come, had been soundly beaten 3–0 by an England side in which the rebels Greig, Knott, Underwood and Woolmer had played prominent parts.

On 16 November, WSC staged its first 'trial' match, which 5,000 spectators attended free of charge. WSC were still wary of establishment litigation. Richie Benaud, who was the most knowledgeable cricket authority among WSC's advisers, announced at a press conference that the 'rules' of WSC cricket would not be those of established cricket, which he pointed out were the copyright of the MCC.

WSC faced other difficulties. Regular cricket arenas were denied them, so they were forced to adapt other available areas of space. Wickets were prepared in an ingenious way. They were cultivated in hot-houses in huge concrete trays which could be transported to the grounds and dropped into place. They proved surprisingly good. Those at the Victorian Football League Park at Melbourne were allowed to stay in place throughout the season at additional cost to WSC. Other Packer innovations were restrictions on field placing (defensive fields were precluded at the start of games) and the introduction of evening games under floodlights.

WSC fielded three teams: Australia, West Indies and the Rest of the World, which was made up of players from England, Pakistan and South Africa. 'Super-Tests' and one-day games were played. Attendances were considerably smaller than WSC hoped. This was partly due, no doubt, to the fact that WSC Australia were generally outplayed by the West Indian and World teams. The four floodlit games at Melbourne's VFL Park were exceptions, being watched by an average of nearly 15,000 per day, which Mr Packer had stated beforehand was a break-even point. The 'Tests', however, despite the large number allowed in free, drew less than half of the spectators which watched the official Test series between Australia and India, which resulted in the narrowest of 3–2 wins for Australia.

The matches were widely promoted on television, with emphasis being placed on the personalities of the players. The nature of the teams made it difficult to engender real enthusiasm over the results. The players were motivated by win bonuses.

Much of the cricket featured a good deal of intimidatory fast bowling.

The cost to Kerry Packer's companies of the first WSC season was estimated to be about £2 million, this being the deficit after advertising revenue and gate receipts had been deducted from an outlay necessarily large to launch the new project. However, it had provided him with 315 hours of cheap television, with reasonable viewing figures.

Meanwhile the England touring party to Pakistan and New Zealand left on 24 November. This was the first tour in which, at the suggestion of the TCCB, the tourists were called 'England' rather than MCC. The Packer players, being unavailable for all the matches, were not considered. The fee for each tourist was raised to £5,000 plus £100 for each previous tour, compared to £3,000 for the 1976–77 tour of India.

After two drawn Tests in Pakistan, Kerry Packer released Imran, Mushtaq and Zaheer from his WSC series to play in the deciding third Test, and they duly arrived in Karachi and appeared in the nets the day before the match. The England players considered withdrawing and thus bringing the series to a premature end if the Packer players were selected. The Pakistan Board announced that they would not play.

The Pakistan Board of Control then had to select the party to tour England in 1978. The Packer players, Majid, Imran, Mushtaq and Zaheer, were not considered because they could not guarantee their availability to play for Pakistan in all future matches. Amid great controversy a meeting was called on 26 March 1978 under the chairmanship of the Chief Martial Law Administrator at which representatives of the game's organization and former Test captains were present. The Administrator ruled that the Packer players should not be included in the party. The England selectors also overlooked the Packer men.

In March 1978 the Australian Board took a similarly hard line in selecting the players to tour the West Indies. The Australian Board were, of course, the least likely to compromise with Packer or his players. Australia sent a completely new team, led by Bobby Simpson, the captain of the mid-1960s, who was brought out of long retirement.

The West Indies, on the other hand, chose their Packer players for the Tests. The West Indian Board had been against the original ICC ban, realising that the financial structure of cricket in the far-flung islands was shaky in the extreme, and that a second eleven Test team would spell disaster. West Indies consequently won the first two Tests easily. They then attempted to experiment with some new players with a view to the forthcoming tour of India, when the Packer players would not be available. For the third Test, D. L. Haynes, R. A. Austin, who had recently signed for Packer, and D. L. Murray, secretary of the West Indies Players' Association, were replaced by non-Packer players. Clive Lloyd resigned as captain in protest, and subsequently the remaining Packer players withdrew. West Indies narrowly lost. The West Indies Board then required from the Packer players an assurance that they would be available for the Indian tour; this was not forthcoming and the West Indies thereafter joined the other affected countries in not considering Packer players for Tests.

In February 1978, the ICC and TCCB had decided not to appeal against the High Court ruling of November. The TCCB stated that, so far as the English counties were concerned, they could not make recommendations about the engagement of WSC players. Six English players were involved: Greig and Snow of Sussex, Knott, Underwood and Woolmer of Kent, and Amiss of Warwickshire, but there were a number of overseas players currently playing for other English Counties, among them Greenidge, Roberts and Barry Richards for Hampshire, and Viv Richards and Garner for Somerset. Kent announced that all their WSC players, including Asif of Pakistan, would be invited to play, and Hampshire and Somerset also re-engaged their overseas players. The English players were all engaged on a year's contract to meet legal requirements, but Alan Knott refused his, preferring to retire from first-class cricket in 1978. Dennis Amiss was under particular pressure. Bob Willis has related that the atmosphere in the Warwickshire dressing room was unhappy, with the committee and the majority of players feeling that Amiss should not 'have his cake and eat it' by playing for both Warwickshire and WSC, and they largely ignored him during matches.

On 25 July 1978, the ICC met at Lords. On the previous

day, David Clark, chairman of the ICC, resigned from the Kent committee after 30 years service. Kent had just announced that new contracts were to be offered to Asif, Woolmer and Underwood, in effect declaring a unilateral 'truce' with their Packer players, and thereby forcing Mr Clark to resign from the club, lest his Kent and ICC duties should lead him to be regarded as 'double-dealing'.

The ICC meeting considered WSC proposals for an amicable co-operation. These proposals had been put to David Clark and Jack Bailey, secretary of MCC, in a meeting with WSC officials held in the United States for secrecy. The proposals involved several series of matches to be played in various parts of the world, beginning with India, New Zealand and Pakistan playing a knock-out series to provide a fourth team to play with Australia, England and West Indies in a 'Super-Test' series, the winners subsequently to play in each of the other countries. There would also be a World XI, comprised presumably of South Africans and players from the countries initially eliminated, to play the four 'Super-Test' countries in a further series of one-day internationals. The ICC predictably rejected these proposals, on the grounds that conventional cricket would be hopelessly disrupted. The ICC nevertheless left the door open for further proposals, and Andrew Caro, the new managing director of WSC, expressed his satisfaction.

Towards the end of the summer, Warwickshire announced that Dennis Amiss would not be retained for the following season. This caused consternation in some Warwickshire members, particularly in the light of the decision of Kent, who won the County Championship, to retain their Packer men. A special General Meeting was arranged for 26 September to discuss the affair.

The Cricketers' Association stepped in at this point. The Association had taken the view that its function was to protect all its members, Packer or not, and that this could best be achieved by striving to bring about a compromise between the two branches of cricket. They advised Amiss that if some such compromise were to be reached during the winter, then Warwickshire would be happy to keep one of their best players – if not, then the situation could be reviewed then. Amiss therefore requested that the meeting be cancelled, and a challenge to Warwickshire's Committee deferred.

In Australia, Jeff Thomson was trying to 'have his cake and eat it'. Having withdrawn from the Packer enterprise, he was regarded as the leading box-office draw in the Australian side for the forthcoming Ashes series of 1978/79. Packer made a further offer and Thomson accepted, leading to the following statement from the Australian Cricket Board:

> It was announced last Friday, September 29, that World Series Cricket had entered into a three-year contract with Mr Jeff Thomson despite its awareness that Mr Thomson had agreed to play only in matches controlled by the Board and state associations during the 1978–79 Australian season, and despite the publicity given to the fact that the Board had refused Mr Thomson's request that he be released from his contractual obligations to the Board.
>
> The Board would naturally have preferred to resolve this matter without resort to the courts and, in order that Mr Thomson's contractural obligations to the Board should be respected, the Board sought an assurance from World Series Cricket that it would not select Mr Thomson to play cricket in any of its teams until after the conclusion of the Australian cricket season on March 31, 1979. World Series Cricket had declined to give such an assurance.

Once more the two sides faced each other in court. Mr Justice Kearney, after a hearing lasting 12 days, held that Thomson was bound by the contract he signed with the Australian Cricket Board earlier in the year, and could not play for WSC before April 1979. The judge criticised some of Thomson's evidence and awarded costs against him and WSC. The victory for the Australian Board promised them little comfort, as Thomson announced that he would spend the Australian summer fishing off Queensland, and would never play for Australia again. It was a measure of the relative strengths of the rivals at the time that whereas WSC would not badly miss Thomson's services, the official Test team would, and although he lost the case, Mr Packer could not be dissatisfied at the outcome.

A recap at the end of the English summer of 1978 showed

therefore that in the English season, which had not yet clashed with WSC games, all of which had been scheduled for the Australian summer, the WSC players were appearing for their Counties, with the exception of Knott, who had declined a one-year contract, while Amiss had been told he would not be retained for 1979. So far as Test cricket was concerned, the West Indies had begun by selecting their Packer men, but had now joined Australia, England and Pakistan in not picking them. India and New Zealand were not yet involved, not having any WSC players, although there were rumours that Mr Packer was seeking to recruit R. J. Hadlee and G. P. Howarth of New Zealand and B. S. Bedi and S. M. Gavaskar of India.

The Test tours due to take place in 1978–79, and thus clash with WSC's second season, were England in Australia, the West Indies in India, India in Pakistan and Pakistan in Australia and New Zealand. Pakistan, whose depleted side had been well-beaten by England in 1978, were the first to break up the united front displayed against the rebels. General K. M. Azhar, head of cricket in Pakistan, announced that should there be no fixture clashes and nothing in the Packer players' contracts to stand in the way, Pakistan would welcome them into the Test team. The players concerned were Asif, Imran, Majid, Mushtaq and Zaheer. Pakistan were no doubt moved by the necessity of doing well against India, and the players in fact turned out against India and in the tour of Australia and New Zealand.

The 1978–79 Australian season was the showdown between conventional cricket and WSC. On the one hand a second-string Australia and a weakened England were playing six Test matches for the Ashes, on the other hand WSC Australia, West Indies and the World XI were presenting their brand of razzma-tazz, macho cricket.

The WSC organization had learned from the disappointing response to its first season, and all sorts of gimmicks were invented to promote the matches of 1978–79. The Channel 9 network set out to sell WSC to Australia. Giveaways, competi-tions, advertisements, sweat-shirts, sponsorship agreements with various products and a theme-song, 'C'mon Aussie, Aussie C'mon' helped to get the massage across. As well as the 'Super Tests' and one-day games, there was a Country Cup, a series which took the players to the outback to spread the word in places which had not seen such distinguished cricketers before.

Mr Packer had been given permission to use the Sydney Cricket Ground, at which he provided free parking for the public, and he also provided free transport to the Waverley ground at Melbourne. The players were built up like film stars, and the matches conducted with something of the violence of a boxing match. The ubiquitous WSC logo (a ball hitting stumps) soon summed up nicely the basic approach, and contrasted revealingly with the Australian Board's marketing device, knights in armour. Fast bowling and repeated bouncers were the order of the day.

The highlight of the WSC season was the first floodlit limited-overs game on the Sydney Cricket Ground. In a first-class arena for the first time, Packer promoted the match as hard as possible, even urging families to take the night out if only to look at the lights. The match was a huge success, and although many were allowed in for nothing, 50,000 attended. As the matches proceeded, and the official Australian Test team began to take a beating, the crowds for WSC cricket remained satisfactorily high, particularly in the traditional cricket centres like Sydney, Melbourne and Brisbane. The crowds were made up of many new supporters, attracted by the bright lights, novelty and ballyhoo, less knowledgable and probably less committed than the diehard fans.

The television coverage by eight cameras was good, catering for new followers by illustrations and explanations of terms like 'in-swinger'. The commentaries were designed to engender excitement at all costs, and Jim Laker, for one, found the descriptions 'magnificent' or 'superb' when applied to quite ordinary play to be tedious.

Packer's second season was a success. Increased revenue, lower costs and a successful television campaign all added up to strengthening WSC's position in relation to conventional cricket. The England tour, by comparison, was a financial disaster.

WSC followed this success by taking the circus to the West Indies. The West Indies Board were facing bankruptcy. When the Packer players had withdrawn from the 1977–78 Georgetown Test, and the series had become virtually a second eleven contest, the season had become a heavy loss. The Board were in even greater trouble in 1978–79. The 'first-team squad' were playing for WSC in Australia, the 'second team squad' were touring India and Sri Lanka. On their return the West Indian season would have to be rushed through, so that many players could resume their county commitments in England.

The West Indian Board had to seek some agreement with Kerry Packer. The territories settled for ground rentals and a portion of the gate, and the Board an ex-gratia payment. So the West Indies accepted co-existence – not Mr Packer's ultimate aim, perhaps, but it further established that his enterprise was well-founded and would not go away without some cost or granting of concessions from the traditional authorities.

The Packer promotional machine again did its work, but there were occasional disturbances and a major hiccup in the fourth 'Super Test', coincidentally at Georgetown, where the Packer contingent had walked out the year before. Trouble arose after a stoppage for rain followed by an assurance from a WSC official that play would commence on time the following day, provided no more rain fell. It didn't, and a capacity crowd waited for play to start. Instead there were the interminable inspections and lack of information that annoy cricket crowds the world over. In Georgetown, there was a riot which wrecked the pavilion, destroyed the club records and forced the teams to cower in the dressing rooms wearing their helmets for protection against missiles.

The tour as a whole was a success, however, with sponsorships, large crowds, profits for WSC and financial relief for the Board.

A meeting of the Cricketers' Association at Edgbaston on April 1979, prior to the new English season, promised conflict between Packer players and the rest. Some of the England party which had toured Australia (and which Mr Packer had challenged to play his Australians at the end of the tour) were known to want the Counties to stop engaging WSC men. There were other proposals which would entail English cricketers refusing to play against Packer men, which would disrupt the forthcoming World Cup, in which Pakistan and the West Indies were proposing to select Packer players. Kerry Packer had threatened to counter any such boycotts of his players by bringing his circus to England.

In the event, however, the Association again decided to mark time. ICC officials had been to Australia to talk to Mr Packer. The Association's President, John Arlott, revealed that the Association had been asked 'not to rock the boat'. A settlement was hoped for in weeks rather than months. The Association was assured that traditional cricket would not be the loser. The Australian Board were to meet on 23 April when the television contract which had provoked the whole Packer affair would be on the agenda. The Association therefore agreed to await events, and in the absence of a settlement in the meantime to meet again on 5 July.

A happy outcome of the anticipated settlement was that Dennis Amiss and Warwickshire were reunited, a triumph for the Association's diplomacy the previous autumn. Alan Knott also returned to first-class cricket for Kent, and Jeff Thomson subsequently returned to cricket and played again for Australia.

The Packer affair seemed to have ended as suddenly as it began when the Australian Cricket Board met on 23 April. Afterwards they announced that they had granted Kerry Packer's Channel 9 exclusive television rights for their matches in Australia, including Test matches. There were reports, unconfirmed, that the agreement was for three years, that the sum involved was £600,000 and the WSC would be disbanded from 31 January 1980.

There was a diehard opinion among cricket followers that Mr Packer's whole operation had been unnecessary, that he would have received the contract at this time anyway and that in the meantime the cost to cricket, both financial and in spirit, had been damaging. The optimistic view was that cricket could now resume in its traditional way, with the additional sponsorship which the Packer intrusion had provoked, like that of the Cornhill company for Test matches, protecting it from future attacks by private entrepreneurs.

This view was shattered a month later when on 30 May the Australian Board announced details of a 10-year agreement with PBL Sports Pty Ltd, a subsidiary of Kerry Packer's Consolidated

Press. The statement of the ACB's chairman, Bob Parish, ran as follows:

> I am pleased to announce that the agreement between the Australian Cricket Board and PBL Sports Pty Ltd. has been signed and will be lodged with the Trade Practices Commissioner.
>
> Under the agreement the Board has granted PBL Sports Pty Ltd. the exclusive right, for a term of ten years, to promote the programme of cricket organised by the Board and to arrange the televising and merchandising in respect of that programme. For the first three years of the agreement the Board has agreed that PBL Sports Pty Ltd may arrange a contract for the televising of the programme with the Channel 9 network.
>
> World Series Cricket Pty Ltd will cease to promote cricket matches in Australia or elsewhere during the term of the agreement. However, under the programme the World Series logo will continue to be worn in international one-day matches by Australian players.
>
> The Australian Board will have the exclusive responsibility for the selection of Australian teams, and has agreed that no player will be excluded from selection by reason only of that player having participated prior to the commencement of the 1979–80 cricket season in any match not authorised by the Board. There will be no change in Board policy that Australian teams will be selected only from those players who participate in Sheffield Shield cricket.
>
> It is envisaged that the programme each season will comprise five or six Test matches and an international one-day series, to be known as the Benson and Hedges World Series Cup, of fifteen matches plus a final which will be the best of five matches. These international matches will involve two overseas teams and the Australian team. The programme will also include the Sheffield Shield competition and a one-day series of nine matches between the states.
>
> Playing conditions of all matches will be under the control of the Board and the Board has agreed to consider favourably the introduction of the 30-yard circle in limited-overs

matches, day/night matches and, on an experimental basis, the use of coloured clothing in Benson and Hedges World Series one-day limited-overs international matches.

The programme for the 1979–80 season will not be finally determined for some weeks. England and India have accepted invitations to come to Australia in 1979–80. The Board has agreed to ask the Indian board to defer their visit until next season, 1980–81, and will invite the West Indian Board to send an official team to participate in the 1979–80 programme.

A basic programme of matches has been prepared by the Board programme committee. All matches will be played on venues as determined by the Board.

The following prize-money will be provided: for each Test – $A10,000 comprising $A6,000 to the winner, $A3,000 to the loser, $A1,000 to the player of the match. For each one-day match – $A5,000 comprising $A3,000 to the winner, $A1,500 to the loser, $A500 to the player of the match. For the one-day final – $A50,000 comprising $32,000 to the winner, $A16,000 to the loser, $A2,000 to the player of the match.

The Board is pleased to advise that the Benson and Hedges company will continue to be the sole and official sponsor of international cricket in Australia, of the Sheffield Shield competition and the Australian team.

Finally, although the Board's cricket sub-committee, first established in September 1976, and which comprises three Board representatives and an elected player representative of each of the six states' practice squads will continue to meet regularly, the Board has agreed that the Australian captain, for the time being, and/or a players' representative elected by the six state representatives, may attend board meetings on request or by invitation to discuss any matters they may wish to discuss or that the Board may wish to discuss with them. The Board will also endeavour to arrange that the captain of a state team and/or the elected players' representative may similarly attend state association meetings.

The Board is unanimously of the opinion that its decision

to accept the proposal from PBL is in the best interests of Australian and international cricket.'

This startling document passed the promotion of Australian cricket from the Board to a private company, which would influence the programme, the rules and the clothing, and had already postponed a tour by India in favour of the more commercial England and West Indies.

Cricket had not been under the control of private hands so much since 1903, when the English touring party to Australia went for the first time under the auspices of MCC, rather than private speculative individuals.

The victory belonged to Kerry Packer's money. The Australian Board had lost heavily during the dispute, with the Ashes tour of 1978–79 being the first to lose money since 1903/04. There was nevertheless considerable dismay, even anger, around the world at the Australian Board's decision. The conflict had been seen originally to concern only the Australians. The ICC had backed the Australian Board in its determination not to accommodate Mr Packer. The sudden capitulation of the Australian Board looked to some to be treachery.

At its annual general meeting at the end of June, the ICC approved the Australian Board's agreement in principle, leaving unresolved details for the Australian Board.

The TCCB, the following day, announced that, in the 1979–80 tour, no more than eleven one-day matches would be played, and that 'no abnormal conditions' would be tolerated, which was taken to mean that England would not play in the coloured clothes that WSC had introduced. They also announced that in the three-match Test series the Ashes would not be at stake, a view greeted with derision in Australia. It was felt that the ACB/PBL agreement did not imply two tours every Australian season, and that in the next 'regular' England tour of 1982–83 the traditional format of five or six Tests would be resumed.

Having 'bought' Australian cricket, a satisfied Kerry Packer retired to the side-lines and allowed his lieutenants to develop the 'product'. Andrew Caro, former WSC head, saw this not as old-fashioned and respectable, but appealing to a new public for whom 'Bradman was the name of a stand'. The new scene was typified by the Series Co-ordinator for 1970–80, a charming young former secretary called Irene Cave, who saw her role as getting 'behinds on seats'. Clearly a new audience was being sought, as well as the old traditional one.

The England side arrived in Australia in November. Derek Underwood was the only WSC cricketer in the party. The English authorities expressed reservations over the one-day rules and the floodlit matches, among them the proposed fines for slow over rates, the use of a white ball, the number of bouncers permitted per over and the availability of practice facilities under floodlights. These doubts were usually expressed by J. M. Brearley, the captain, who also declined to wear striped clothing, and who was consequently roughly treated by the Australian press. The tour was a little rough, too. Ian Chappell, of South Australia, put nine men on the leg side when bowling to Brearley in contempt of Brearley and England's distaste for restrictions on placing fielders. Dennis Lillee often taunted Brearley and attempted to bat in a Test match with an aluminium bat, to which Brearley objected. These incidents encouraged the crowds to follow the press line and abuse Brearley at every opportunity. The new cricket did not impress the tourists, most of whom thought the tour best forgotten. W. J. O'Reilly, the former Australian bowler, also thought the season, for a number of reasons, the most unsatisfactory Australian cricket experience in 68 years, referring back to the ill-fated triangular Test series in England in 1912.

In the Australian season 1980–81, India and New Zealand toured Australia, and a programme of 20 one-day Benson and Hedges matches were played, as envisaged in the agreement between the Australian Board and the Packer empire quoted earlier. The last match, played before a world record limited-overs crowd of 52,990, ended in uproar when Trevor Chappell bowled the final delivery along the ground, to ensure New Zealand would not score the six needed for victory. The Australians won $A130,000 of the season's prize-money, but cricket lost a little more of its traditional appeal.

In 1981–82 West Indies and Pakistan joined Australia in the 20-match one-day series. Lynton Taylor, Managing Director of

PBL, still marketing and promoting all cricket in Australia, was reported as saying that he did not believe Test cricket could survive in its present format, and that major changes would be necessary to hold public interest. Over 100,000 who watched the Adelaide Test apparently gave him the lie, but the news was disquieting.

England were back in Australia again in 1982–83. The TCCB comments on the signing of the agreement with Packer will be recalled. The requirement that the traditional format of Test matches would be restored came about, as there was a five-match rubber. The one-day programme was as heavy as ever, however, with New Zealand joining in a preliminary programme of 15 matches, with a three-match final to follow. England agreed to play in coloured flannels, turning out in sky-blue in what the English newspapers derisively called 'the pyjama game'.

The array of Channel 9 gimmicks were present. Tony Greig, who had emigrated to Australia to become managing director of an insurance company set up by Kerry Packer, previewed each day's play on television with an array of instruments on the pitch designed to reveal everything about wicket and weather. The Channel 9 publicity presented the series almost as if it were war, and caricatured the English as boasting, super-cilious and effete. When the Australian bowler Terry Alderman was injured in the first Test scuffling with pitch invaders, it was suggested that the advance partisan publicity might have contributed to the crowd skirmishes which followed.

From mid-1979, when the Australian Control Board and Kerry Packer reached agreement, the name of Kerry Packer began to disappear from the headlines. However, the agreement is for ten years, and the influence of the 'Packer revolution' is likely to last longer than that.

Its effects have transformed the Australian season. Two visiting sides are the norm. Floodlit night cricket has been intro-duced. There is a proliferation of one-day internationals in triangular tournaments, which last for up to 20 matches. Coloured flannels have replaced the traditional whites.

Cricket followers have two views of all this, as of the tele-vision coverage, where the camera work has certainly improved, but the success of the commentaries, gadgetry and general tone is debatable. The advertising slots during play, which are particularly intrusive in cricket, are an unavoidable evil.

A new audience has been attracted, which is good in itself, but it is not certain that it will prove a faithful audience, and some of the old audience has been alienated. That some of the new audience might have been attracted by the hyping promotion and the element of needle which has crept into the game, most would regret. Incidents on the field in post-Packer days have mostly involved naturally aggressive cricketers who might well have provoked controversy in any case. There is a feeling, however, that the Australian authorities have become more lenient in dealing with 'offenders'.

Financially, cricketers, and, despite the cost of legal battles, the game itself, have benefitted, not only through the money invested by the Packer companies but by the sponsorship which the traditional game attracted to counter the Packer intrusion.

Perhaps the aspect of the affair which most carries the seeds of lasting change is the concession of the ACB to the Packer group of the promotion and merchandising of the cricket programme in Australia. Andrew Caro, former WSC managing director, suggested in 1979 that if WSC were successful, the focal point of cricket could move from Lord's to Sydney. This might as yet be unlikely, but a powerful influence on the game now exists outside the traditional ruling bodies. So far as Kerry Packer is concerned

> The ball he threw while playing in the park
> Has not yet reached the ground.

9   The Yorkshire Hubbub

The fall of Boycott from Olympus is tragedy of a Homeric order. Despite his brilliant achievements he has offended the gods by simple arrogance and is now bent low. He will wonder today why his prolific 44,210 runs, his 139 centuries, unequalled by Hutton and surpassed in Yorkshire only by Herbert Sutcliffe, find so few admirers. He may muse that genius, if that is what he has, is its own reward. These questions have answers and the superficial ones – that Boycott is a plodder, a poor sport and perhaps a bit of a four-letter fellow in private – miss the real malaise that afflicts his cricket. The truth is that Boycott is a supreme professional and exemplifies in extreme form, the modern game. He is, in a phrase the apotheosis of professional cricket. What is wrong in him begins with what is wrong with it.

The matter of the dismissal of Boycott by the Yorkshire Committee was thought so serious that the *Daily Telegraph* of 5 October 1983 devoted its lead Editorial to the subject and the above is the first of its three paragraphs. The other two paragraphs hark back to the days of Grace, MacLaren, the Hon. F. S. Jackson and Prince Ranjitsinjhi – the old 'amateur' masters, whose only post-war counterparts have been May and Cowdrey.

One can only wonder how much longer writers will drag up cricketers of the so-called 'Golden Age' and compare them with modern players – can there be anyone living who actually witnessed the 'Golden Age', *circa* 1902? The Editor must surely have his tongue in his cheek.

The Yorkshire Hubbub has been bubbling nicely for a quarter

of a century and has fundamentally nothing to do with the hackneyed Gentlemen versus Players argument – at least not in the context of the dashing carefree, debonair amateur against the dour, watch-my-average, pro. The latter confrontation is more related to the classic North versus South struggle – the grit and determination opposed to the dilettante.

The problems associated with Boycott and the Yorkshire Committee go back to the days before the 'Golden Age' to the 1880s or thereabouts.

The Yorkshire team of the day was captained by Tom Emmett, a fast left-hand bowler and professional. Under him were, usually, ten other professionals. The great match of 1880 was against Nottinghamshire on the old Bramall Lane ground at Sheffield. Not an amateur in sight, for Notts were also eleven paid players – but 20,000 came to watch the match, 20,000 who were innocent of the fact that cricket was nothing without the amateur spirit. The *Wisden* report notes: 'No contests are so popular in the North as those between Notts and Yorkshire and an immense throng of people assembled on each of the first two days.'

They came to watch a serious cricket match, not the amateur Southern version of the game: less than 400 runs were scored on the first two days, with Billy Barnes' 34 the highest individual innings. Yorkshire won by five wickets; the only time Notts, the County Champions, were defeated during the season. Ted Peate, Yorkshire's slow left-arm spinner, took 7 for 66, whilst his partner, Billy Bates, renowned for his sartorial elegance, picked up 10 for 68. Old Mary Ann – or Ephraim Lockwood – held the Yorkshire batting together in the first innings after both openers had been dismissed without scoring, whilst Louis Hall took the side to victory in the second innings. The days of professional innocence were however soon to be shattered.

J. M. Kilburn commences Chapter 2 of his Yorkshire History:

Martin Bladen Hawke was introduced into Yorkshire county cricket by favouritism. He was invited to play in the Scarborough Festival, or Carnival, as it was then known, by the Reverend E. S. Carter, who arranged Festival teams. Canon Carter was also a moving spirit in the Yorkshire Gentleman

CC, based on York, and there he had noted Hawke's enthusiasm, ability and, perhaps most significantly, his availability. The Hon M. B. Hawke was awarded a cricket 'Blue' at Cambridge in 1882 and joined Yorkshire when the university term ended. He was invited, no doubt in accordance with the social decencies, to act as captain, but he declined, saying to Emmett: 'I prefer to play under you and pick up a few wrinkles.'

Hawke's Yorkshire debut came in 1881, when he appeared in the two September matches at Scarborough – neither of the matches could be described as representative Yorkshire games, for in both cases half the team were local amateurs. MCC beat them by an innings, and a mish-mash of amateurs representing the I Zingari, in the second game, won by 159 runs. Hawke's regular County cricket began midway through 1882 after the University match on 28 June, and he took over as captain after the University match of the following year. It was the beginning of a 28-year reign, a span only equalled by the immortal W. G. Grace, but unlike the Doctor, Hawke was scarcely worth his place in the side, except as 'captain'. It is true that in his 31 seasons of first-class cricket he scored 16,000 runs, but his average was just over 20 – the only other players to top 10,000 runs with so low an average were famous bowlers or wicket-keepers, Tony Lock, Godfrey Evans and the like. Hawke was no bowler or wicketkeeper.

A more significant difference between Hawke and Grace was that the Gloucestershire side of the 1880s contained as a rule one professional and ten amateurs – with the introduction of Hawke, Yorkshire were one amateur and ten professionals. It was not long before his rule turned to paternalistic benevolence. His first step was to 'clean up' the eleven. A number of players on the edge of the County team found their chances of a permanent place blocked because of their 'manners', and in 1887 Hawke moved against the Test cricketer, Ted Peate. Peate was born in 1856, began his first class career in 1879, and gained a regular place in the County team of 1880 – his record in English first-class cricket from 1880 to 1886 was so brilliant it deserves publishing if only to demonstrate the standing of the cricketer whom Hawke demolished:

	M	Overs	Mdns	Runs	Wkts	Avge
1880	22	1314.3	581	1662	138	12.04
1881	27	1712	760	2195	173	12.68
1882	30	1562.1	864	2466	214	11.52
1883	27	1376.3	665	1753	120	14.60
1884	30	1564	788	1868	137	13.63
1885	24	1699	903	1945	115	16.91
1886	20	980.2	542	1027	70	14.67

Just one further statistic to show Peate's ability – some 200 bowlers have taken over 1,000 first-class wickets, but only five of them at a lower average than Peate's record of 13.48.

The magazine *Cricket Chat* described Peate: 'he was a genial good natured mortal who makes the best of life; a hearty, honest Yorkshireman and proud of it.'

Peate's happy-go-lucky attitude was all too much for Lord Hawke and one escapade too many at the start of the 1887 season brought a premature end to the greatest Yorkshire bowler of the decade.

Lord Hawke – was it a coincidence that he succeeded to the title in 1887? – noted many years later in his book of reminiscences:

> One of my saddest tasks was to dismiss him [Peate] from the Yorkshire eleven. But he bore me no grudge, and whenever I subsequently ran across him, invariably he greeted me with the old familiar smile and the same slow, spontaneous: 'Good morning, my Lord. I hope you are as well as I am.'

Since Lord Hawke deprived Peate of a possible ten years of county cricket with the additional possibilities of playing for England and of touring overseas, one wonders exactly how sincere his greetings to his Lordship were in later years.

By the end of the 1880s, Lord Hawke was Yorkshire cricket. If he was hard on Peate, he was generous to other Yorkshire players. John Thewlis, a noted batsman of the 1860s, was discovered in 1898, aged 70, reduced to carrying coals in Manchester for a few pence. He was going blind and he stated: 'I have lost my teeth, but perhaps it's as well, for there hasn't been much for them to do lately.' When the news of Thewlis's poverty reached Lord Hawke, he arranged for the old batsman to be brought back to his native village and to receive a pension.

Lord Hawke abolished talent money, which was automatically paid to the professionals if they hit a fifty or took 6 wickets. He introduced his 'Mark Book', in which he gave merit marks to the players, a system which of course worked two ways. He also brought in winter pay for the professionals, and even saw that the scorer was on half-pay.

Lord Hawke noted: 'This was a new departure and one which I believe has been of incalculable value, not only to the men themselves, in enabling them to maintain themselves adequately, but it has assisted them to withstand temptation . . .'

His autocratic rule naturally increased with the years. Bobby Peel, another England slow bowler, was a second famous cricketer to be drummed out of the eleven. Peel in the middle of 1897 arrived on the field drunk. Lord Hawke ordered him off. Peel's response was to take the ball and proceed to bowl what he assumed would be a perfect delivery. Peel ran up to the wicket and bowled. Unfortunately he failed to realise that he was the wrong way round and the ball sped away to the boundary. Lord Hawke took Peel firmly by the arm and led him off the field and out of county cricket. 'It had to be done for the sake of discipline and for the good of cricket,' commented Hawke, but he admitted that sacking the team's best all-rounder lost Yorkshire the Championship – after 14 years, Hawke, in 1896, had led Yorkshire to the title for the first time.

In July 1898, M. J. Ellison, who was the father of Yorkshire County cricket, died. He had been President of the County Club for 32 years and his place was taken by Lord Hawke. Thus his Lordship held the dual roles of captain and president. His hold on the reins of power were complete and were to remain so until his death in 1938. Is it of significance that the two propagators of the Law that only the Yorkshire-born can play for the County, were both born elsewhere – Ellison in Nottinghamshire and Lord Hawke in Lincolnshire? The Hawke family originally came from Cornwall.

Although it took Lord Hawke the best part of twenty years to perfect his version of County cricket, it can be certainly said that once established, with himself at the helm, the White Rose dominated the Championship for 40 years.

By the time age was loosening Hawke's grip, a successor to the chair of paternal benevolence had been found in Brian Sellers. He took over the captaincy in 1933. Most of the captains between Hawke and Sellers were cricketing nonenities, but that did not matter because Hawke was a firm President and had drilled his professionals from infancy. The old brand of Emmetts, Peates, Peels and Lockwoods had long since vanished from the county scene. Sellers, it might have been assumed, would be another nonenity – his father was the Chairman of the Yorkshire Selection Committee. As Peter Thomas notes in his biographical sketch:

> Sellers demanded that he was not only to be known as captain but seen to be captain. He rigorously set about asserting his will and disciplinarian methods were resented in certain quarters. But it was not discipline for discipline's sake; nor was it to show everyone who was boss; rather it emanated from an almost fanatical thrust and drive to see Yorkshire on top.

The Yorkshire side of the 1930s was most successful. Sellers won the Championship in his first season and ended the 1930s with a hat-trick. Social changes after the Second World War were however much more pronounced than they had been in 1919. Paternalism was no longer to be tolerated.

J. M. Kilburn in *A History of Yorkshire Cricket* explains the position of players in the 1950s:

> Success was edged away from being its own satisfaction. It came to be viewed with an eye on its consequences, those consequences measured carefully in commerical terms. The appeal of a cricketing career involved increasing concern for the material rewards. Invitations to play brought demands for 'caps' or contracts. County effort was related, consciously

or subconsciously, to its effect on publicity for Test-selection purposes. Tests and tours were valued in proportion to off-the-field perquisities obtainable from them.

Almost imperceptibly at first, some of the play became conditioned by some of the extrinsic factors involved. With money at stake and known to be at stake for specified performances a dropped catch or a running misjudgement assumed a significance beyond the course of a match. Prominence through misbehaviour could be more profitable than conscientious obscurity. County cricket opened the way to the artificially stimulated glamour of Test cricket and Test cricket led to commercial careers outside cricket. Cricket was coming to be used by cricketers as a means to an end beyond cricket.

In such an atmosphere the cricket field and the dressing room began to lose attraction or to gain attraction, according to viewpoint. Extension of television and a redirection of much cricket writing towards the cult of personality helped to shift the focus of loyalties from the corporate to the individual. The prevailing national philosophy crudely summarised in 'I'm all right, Jack . . .' infected cricket.

In this period came an explosion of self-interests exemplified in the sale of names and faces for the advertisement of commercial products having no connection with cricket. In this period came the extension of the 'ghosted' book and newspaper article from technical subjects to gossip and concoction of controversy. In this period came the translation of Test matches from games of cricket to concerns of national prestige. Any series must ostensibly be rated the equal of all others and therefore given the same terms of contest; five days for all and every match 'the greatest'.

Emphasis on the individual, glorification of the Test in tinsel trappings and diversification of personal interests all tended to detract from the appeal of county cricket in its day-to-day existence. Some players, no doubt unwittingly, began to think and talk about 'my' performance as distinct from 'our' performance and its consequences. Other players tended to resent egotism; foolish words were spoken and written for publication and harsh ones occasionally passed on the field and in the dressing-rooms. The eventual outcome in Yorkshire was dramatic.

Both Len Hutton and Norman Yardley, Yorkshire's England players, retired from County cricket two or three years early, because they were tired of the new atmosphere that had been created. Many years later Ray Illingworth in his autobiography gave some dramatic accounts of the traumas of a young cricketer in the Yorkshire team of the 1950s. The public at large however were not aware of the problems until 1958, when the 'Wardle Incident' burst into headlines.

Johnny Wardle, the Yorkshire and England spin bowler, was asked if he would be available to tour Australia, if chosen, and was in two minds because he did not wish to leave his family. A business man then announced that he would pay for Wardle's wife to go to Australia. This offer became public and was the cause of some adverse comments. On 27 July the team was announced and included Wardle. Three days later the Yorkshire County Cricket Club issued the following statement:

> The Yorkshire Committee have informed J. H. Wardle that they will not be calling on his services after the end of the season.

Nothing more was said, but on 2 August when the Yorkshire team, with Wardle, were at Old Trafford for the start of the Bank Holiday match against Lancashire, J. R. Burnet, the Yorkshire captain, suddenly announced:

> J. H. Wardle has requested that he stand down from the match because of comments he intends to make about his colleagues in a newspaper article to be published while the match is in progress. He has been given permission to stand down and has left the ground.

The *Daily Mail* then came out with: 'The Most Outspoken Cricket Series of Modern Times: Why I was Sacked by Johnny Wardle'.

The basis of Wardle's articles was that the Yorkshire Committee were crazy to have picked Burnet, a club cricketer who had never appeared in a first-class game, as captain of the team in 1958. Wardle was the senior professional and claimed that every time he offered Burnet advice, the captain either merely ignored him or deliberately took the opposite point of view. At one juncture, when Burnet told the team that more effort was needed, Wardle replied that the only thing wrong with the side was the captain. Wardle continued:

> For years I have said that Yorkshire is run by a lot of people who think that their old-fashioned methods are good enough to cope with modern cricket. A rot has set in with Yorkshire. And it's eating away the greatest county club in the world. If it's going to be stopped they must have new and virile leadership both in the committee-room and on the field. Yorkshire needs new ideas, new blood, and a spirit of adventure.

Wardle's recipe for success was to appoint Phil Sharpe, the 22-year-old batsman, as captain. He went on in further articles to be extremely critical of the Committee and the coaching methods used by the County.

The reaction from the Yorkshire Committee came immediately:

> Wardle broke his contract when he wrote those articles without first obtaining permission, and the committee are therefore terminating his engagement forthwith. In past years Wardle has been warned on several occasions that his general behaviour on the field and in the dressing room left much to be desired. As no improvement was shown this year the decision to dispense with his services was made, as it was unanimously considered essential to have discipline and a happy and loyal team before any lasting improvement could be expected in the play of the Yorkshire XI. It is felt that Wardle's recent articles fully justify the committee's decision.

The problem now moved to Lord's – would the MCC withdraw their invitation to Wardle to tour Australia? Denis Compton in the *Sunday Express* made the following point:

> It seems that the difficulties between Johnny Wardle and the Yorkshire Committee did not arise yesterday or the day

before or the day before that. It was a cloud which had long hung darkly on that horizon. It is plain from everything that has been written and said that for a long time people in the know must have been aware that something of the kind that has happened would happen. In these circumstances is it unreasonable to speculate that the Yorkshire committee knew that they were going to get rid of Wardle – and, of course, knew the precise reason why – before the MCC Committee met on July 27 to choose the party to go to Australia?

The MCC duly met and withdrew their invitation to Wardle. The controversial spinner left first-class cricket for good. If his departure had been an isolated incident it would have been little more than a nine-day wonder, but at the end of the previous summer the Yorkshire Committee had decided to dispense with the services of Willie Watson, the England left-hand batsman. He moved to Leicestershire, where he flourished and regained his place in the Test team – so much so that he was one of the party MCC chose to go to Australia in the winter of 1958–59. Ron Appleyard and Frank Lowson, two other Yorkshire and England cricketers, aged 34 and 33, were both released at the close of the 1958 season, though ill-health played its part in the committee's decisions in both their cases. In two years therefore the team lost four Test Players.

Brian Sellers, the old captain and a power behind the scenes ever since he retired in 1947, was appointed Chairman of the Cricket Committee in 1959 and the young eleven, still under Burnet, won the County Championship – much to the surprise of all the detractors. When the Committee broke the precedent in 1960 and appointed J. V. Wilson captain, the first professional to lead the side since Lord Hawke took the reins from Emmett back in 1883, the Championship was won for the second year in succession.

On the surface therefore peace and prosperity had been restored – the malcontents removed. But Brian Close was not too happy with the new arrangements. Close, who had been the Wonder Boy of County cricket when as an 18-year-old he performed the 'double' of 1,000 runs and 100 wickets in 1949, was now Wilson's understudy and hardly full of admiration for his new captain:

> Vic Wilson was a sound solid citizen in country cricketing terms. He made a lot of runs for Yorkshire – 27 centuries, two double centuries, well over 20,000 runs in all – and was an excellent close-to-the-wicket fielder, especially at leg-slip. He was a quiet man with his own interests and at the end of a day's play he was the first to pack his gear and slip unobtrusively away. Not for him a pint or two in the club or your hotel bar, and an evening's chat ranging over the past day's play and the battle still to come. A quiet man in every way, Vic. We never knew what became of him when the day's toil was over. Certainly he wasn't talking cricket with his men and it was a fair bet that he wasn't thinking cricket, either. In fact in almost every way Vic was too introverted. Maybe he wasn't sure of himself, or of others.

Close was not a quiet critic and ever ready to offer Wilson sage advice. In the end Wilson's response was: 'If you open your mouth just once more, I'll send you home on the train.' According to Close, Wilson's sole idea of tactics was to bowl Fred Trueman until he could hardly stand – and if that didn't work at least the team had tried!

Wilson retired after two summers in charge and the Committee picked Close to take over. Close led Yorkshire to five Championships and was chosen to captain England.

So far as the County was concerned the next trouble came in 1968 when Close was accused of 'misappropriating funds intended for the Yorkshire team'. The rumour proved totally unfounded, but Close determined to discover who started the accusation. Close suspected Fred Trueman on the grounds that the fast bowler had his eyes on the captaincy. Close said as much to the Committee, and Burnet, the old captain, denied that it was Trueman, but Close was not convinced. Illingworth and Binks, the wicketkeeper, agreed with Close. Close's next action was to go back to the Committee and demand that Trueman be retired – Trueman went.

Unfortunately for Close, his best ally, Illingworth, was also at loggerheads with the committee. The paternalism of Lord

Hawke lived on in Brian Sellers and the Yorkshire Committee, so much so that Yorkshire, unlike other counties, did not give players contracts for three or four-year periods. The players lived almost hand to mouth relying on the goodwill of the Committee. Illingworth's place in the side was being challenged by young Geoff Cope and Illingworth, in his late thirties, was worrying about his future. Mike Stevenson in his biography of Illingworth describes the final contretemps:

The crisis was precipitated by a visit to John Nash, the Yorkshire secretary, in which Illy asked if it were true that Geoff Cope was going to be pushed in front of him. 'If so,' he said, 'that's okay. Give me my release and I'll be happy to go. But please don't mess me about for a year and then sack me when I've missed the chance of getting a three or four year contract with somebody else.' John Nash denied that there was any chance of Ray's fears proving to be reality, but he was far from convinced. Eventually he was assured that the committee would never grant him a contract. The fateful letter was written and at once released to the press by Sellers before the Committee had had any chance of discussion or possible modification of their views. It was during a match at Bradford that Bill Bowes arrived in the Yorkshire dressing-room and asked Ray if it was correct that he was leaving. Illy's reaction was immediate 'How the hell do you know? The letter's only been in half-an-hour.'

'Mr. Nash had rung Sellers and Sellers says that you can go and any bugger else that wants to can go with you. He's asked me to handle the press side of things.'

Feelings were sufficiently high on the subject of contracts for several of the senior players to say that they would back Ray to the extent of not playing under certain circumstances. The whole unsavoury affair certainly ended happily for its principal participant but with the somewhat tarnished image of democracy further dented in the county club. It was not as if this was the only time that Sellers acted without the authority of his committee. Members were thoroughly in awe of him so that what he said was law.

The basic point was that Illy's letter of 'resignation' was

conditional upon the committee's final decision to refuse him the contract and the security he demanded. In fact that decision was made by one autocratic individual with whom Ray had on at least one occasion rowed more or less violently and who appeared to be backing a less experienced bowler, prematurely, to usurp his place. It is perfectly possible that the committee, if they had seen that Illingworth and those senior players (Boycott, Trueman and Close among them who supported him wholeheartedly) really meant business, would have reconsidered their refusal to give contracts; but they had been utterly pre-empted by Sellers.

So Illingworth went off to Leicestershire and success both with that County and with England. The following year Jimmy Binks, the wicketkeeper, decided that he had had enough of the county scene and went into premature retirement, but his departure and even that of Illingworth was nothing compared with the explosion after the 1970 season.

In November Close was summoned to what he believed to be a Committee Meeting, but on arrival he discovered only the Secretary and Mr Sellers were present. 'Well Brian,' said Mr Sellers, 'You've had a good innings. I'm giving you the option of resigning or getting the sack.'

Initially Close opted to resign, but on the advice of his supporters changed his mind and the words began to fly. An action group was formed and various meetings held. The Committee announced that they had had to sack Close because he wasn't fit, because he didn't encourage young players and because he did not like one-day cricket. *The Cricketer* commented:

> It seems, on the face of it, to have been a clumsy and bungled business, not least because it looks as if even Yorkshire are throwing their cloth bonnets after the siren of one-day cricket. I don't think we have heard the last of either Close or the Yorkshire Committee who disposed of him.

On 30 January 1971, the Yorkshire Annual General Meeting was held and the Action Group won the day, defeating the Committee's Annual Report by 570 votes to 507. In theory the Committee had two options, to resign or to call a Special

General Meeting. In fact Close moved to Somerset, and the Yorkshire Committee remained unchanged, but spent 1971 making so many experiments with the team, now under Boycott's captaincy, that W. E. Bowes, the old Test bowler, at the end of the summer noted:

> Yorkshire had the worst season in their history. A win by 19 points in the last match against Northamptonshire – ending the longest sequence of 17 matches without a victory the county has ever known – lifted them to thirteenth place . . . Unquestionably the loss of such a talented cricketer and knowledgeable captain as Close could not fail to have an adverse influence on the team – and in three different ways. Firstly, the formation of an Action Group of members, criticising and seeking a vote of no confidence in the Committee and calling for a better relationship between selectors and players, produced perhaps a weakening of decisions. If a young player asked to leave Yorkshire for a trial with another county, steps were taken to keep him. Yorkshire promised trials and gave financial inducements. It was a policy a long way removed from that which contended that Yorkshire did not want a player who was not prepared to fight for a place in the side and then fight to keep it.

The major change in the affairs of the Club was not however the disappearance of Close, or the apparent shift of emphasis by the Committee, but the retirement as Chairman of Brian Sellers in 1972. Ninety years of strong, if controversial and outspoken, leadership had ended, for Sellers had inherited the mantle of Lord Hawke. Both men had made mistakes and enemies, but they had served Yorkshire well, and the tally of thirty County Championship titles won under their combined patronage was a fitting epitaph to their memories. The past decade is a story of muddle and indecision, of a house divided and a consequent lack of success.

For several years after Sellers left, ill-feeling grew among the players and Committee, but it was not until 1977 that the press began to stir. Don Brennan, the old England and Yorkshire wicketkeeper, and Yorkshire Committee member, began a campaign to remove Boycott from the captaincy. He put up

Geoff Cope as an alternative. A Committee Meeting was held in November, at which Brennan's proposals came to nothing. He resigned forthwith and the Committee re-appointed Boycott captain for 1978. The Committee however had further plans and they announced the appointment of Illingworth (captain of Leicestershire) as manager to commence in 1979.

This naturally produced a howl of protest from Leicestershire, but that was muted compared with the concern of the more erudite Yorkshire supporters, who forecast trouble between Illingworth the manager and Boycott the captain. The Committee also announced the abolition of the Yorkshire Selection Committee and stated that from 1979 the teams would be chosen by the captain and manager.

Season 1978 proved to be a much better one for the County and they rose from twelfth to fourth place in the Championship. The anti-Boycott faction which had developed from Brennan and his acolytes became loud and well-orchestrated. Their statisticians quickly proved that Yorkshire's 1978 success was nothing to do with the captain, but was due to John Hampshire, the man who led Yorkshire when Boycott was away playing for England. This time the anti-Boycott lobby won the day. At a Committee Meeting on 29 September, the following statement was issued:

> In the interests of the Club the Committee has decided to offer the captaincy to J. H. Hampshire. It was hoped that G. Boycott would accept the two year contract which was offered to him.

No reason for the change was given. There had however been much publicity for the Yorkshire match at Northampton, when apparently in retaliation for a slow century by Boycott, Hampshire and Johnson had 'deliberately' scored 11 off the final 10 overs (prior to the closure at 100 overs) to prevent the County obtaining an extra batting bonus point. A lengthy enquiry into this incident by the Yorkshire Selection Committee seemed to achieve nothing.

On 9 December 1978, the pro-Boycott Reform Group forced the Club to hold a Special Meeting at Harrogate. There were three items on the Agenda:

1. Vote of Confidence in the Committee
2. Recommending the resignation of the Cricket Committee
3. The re-appointment of Boycott as captain

The press and television coverage of the pros and cons was enormous, but on the day the postal votes decided the issues and the eloquence of the pro-Boycott speakers counted for little, all the motions going against them. Boycott bowed to the electorate and signed the offered two-year contract.

The new era under the Illingworth-Hampshire regime did not however produce any improvement in the playing results of the County, who in fact dropped three places in the Championship. Hampshire proved no more effective as captain than Boycott and the pro-Boycott Reform Group were quick to point this out. The disarray behind the scenes cried out for a strong man to point the way and clear out the miscreants.

Season 1980 brought little relief for Yorkshire's supporters. Hampshire tired of being pig-in-the-middle, resigned as captain, moved to Derbyshire and published his reminiscences, which only proved that he was naive and did nothing to heal the wounds. The Committee wobbled on the fence and took another backward step by appointing Chris Old, the England seam bowler, to lead the County. Old was totally ineffective. Illingworth tried to promote the young Neil Hartley as vice-captain. A campaign to dismiss Illingworth began to find adherents and Boycott was suspended for publicly criticising Illingworth.

If 1981 was grim, 1982 proved if anything worse. In mid season Old was sacked from the captaincy. Hartley's candidature for the leadership collapsed because he was unable to maintain a place in the first eleven. So, amid great trumpetings from the press, Illingworth came out of retirement to skipper the side. In view of the complete disharmony among players, committee and supporters, it was surprising that the team managed to hold on to tenth place in the Championship.

During the 1983 season scarcely a week passed without rumours of more unrest, usually concerning one of the younger players who couldn't stand the friction any longer and wished to move to calmer waters. The year was, from the playing viewpoint, to prove the most disastrous of them all, with Yorkshire at the foot of the Championship table. On 3 October 1983 came the headline 'Geoff Boycott Dismissed by Yorkshire'. The Chairman of the cricket sub-committee, none other than J. R. Burnet, the captain who had been attacked by Johnny Wardle 25 years before, announced:

> The Committee felt the time had come to make major decisions. We cannot go any lower. The rancour and controversy of recent years must end.

D. L. Bairstow, the wicketkeeper, was appointed captain for 1984, with Illingworth remaining as manager. To confound their critics the Committee had granted Boycott a Testimonial for 1984, before wielding the axe. The pro-Boycott Group rallied to his support, demanding a Special Meeting to censure the Committee.

The Special Meeting of the County Club was held at Harrogate on 21 January 1984. The members were invited to vote on three resolutions:

1. That Boycott should be reinstated;
2. No confidence in the Committee;
3. No confidence in the Cricket Committee.

The pro-Boycott group, led by Sid Fielden, won all three resolutions, the voting being as follows: 4155–3109, 3609–3578 and 3997–3209. After a brief hesistation, the Committee resigned *en bloc*; Yorkshire members however had a chance to reconsider this condemnation of the Committee when new elections were held prior to the Annual General Meeting.

It is a story as yet without an end, but one which points to the value of having one powerful figure to control the destiny of a County Club, rather than the compromises produced by 'Committee-cricket'.

Index

The letter P indicates that the subject is illustrated between pages 96 and 97

Index

Index

Oldfield, W. A. S. 82, 84, 99, P
O'Reilly, W. J. 79, 82, 154
Oscroft, W. 28 *et seq*
Oxenham, R. K. 76

Packer, Kerry 20, 129 *et seq*, P
Packer, Sir Frank 129
Palairet, R. C. N. 75, 81, 83, 89
Pamensky, Joe, 127
Parish, Bob 151
Parr, William 20, 21, 23
Parry, D. R. 126
Pascoe, L. S. 132
Pataudi, Nawab of 75, 79, 84, 88
Paynter, E. 75, 87
Pearson, D. B. 103, 106
Peate, E. 158, 159, 160, 162
Peel, R. 161, 162
Perkins, H. 32, 46
Perrin, P. A. 74
Phillips, John 54
Phillipson, W. E. 108
Pilch, F. 40
Pollard, V. 12
Pollock, R. G. 132
Ponsford, W. H. 77, 87
Ponsonby, F. 46
Pooley, E. 28 *et seq*
Price, W. F. F. 100, 101, 102
Prideaux, R. M. 115
Procter, M. J. 132, 137 *et seq*

Rae, A. F. 126
Ranjitsinjhi, Prince 157
Ransford, V. S. 64, P
Redpath, I. R. 112, 132, 138
Rhodes, H. J. 106 *et seq*
Richards, B. A. 132, 144
Richards, I. V. A. 125, 132, 144
Roberts, A. M. E. 132, 144

Robertson, Dr. A. 87
Robins, D. H. 125, 128
Robins, R. W. V. 75
Robinson, R. D. 132
Root, C. F. 73
Rorke, G. F. 103, 104
Rowe, L. G. 126, P
Ryder, J. 81

Saunders, J. 40, 41
Searle, W. 40
Selby, J. 28 *et seq*
Sellers, A. B. 162, 166, 168, P
Sharpe, P. J. 165
Shaw, A. 28 *et seq*, P
Sheppard, Rev D. S. 115, 118
Short, Peter 139
Shrewsbury, A. 28 *et seq*, P
Silk, D. W. R. 116
Simpson, R. B. 143
Slade, Mr. Justice, 137 *et seq*
Slater, K. N. 103, 104, 112
Smith, D. 71
Smith, H. A. 92
Smith, M. J. K. 109
Snow, J. A. 132, 137 *et seq*
Sobers, G. St. A. 102, 125
Spofforth, F. R. 54
Statham, J. B. 103
Steele, Raymond 139
Stephenson, F. daC. 126
Stephenson, H. H. 20
Sutcliffe, H. 75, 80, 157

Tarrant, G. 24
Tate, M. W. 75
Taylor, Lynton 135, 140, 154
Tennyson, L. H. 84
Thewlis, J. 160
Thomas, J. H. 86
Thoms, Robert 45, 50
Thomson, J. R. 132, 137, 146, 150
Trotman, E. T. 126

Trueman, F. S. 109, 167, 169
Trumper, V. T. 62 *et seq*, P
Tull, Louis 128
Tunks, W. 56
Turnbull, M. J. C. 75
Tyldesley, E. 84
Tyson, F. H. 103

Ulyett, Roy 108
Underwood, D. L. 124, 132, 138, 139, 144, 145

Venn, Rev H. 11
Verity, H. 75, 78, 87
Voce, W. 35, 74 *et seq*, P

Walcott, H. 102
Walker, M. H. N. 132
Walker, P. M. 109
Walker, T. 37
Wall, T. W. 77
Walters, K. D. 132
Ward, William 41
Wardill, R. W. 57
Wardle, J. H. 164 *et seq*, P
Warner, P. F. 74 *et seq*
Watson, F. 92
Watson, W. 166
Willes, John 38, 39
Willey, P. 124
Willis, R. G. D. 125, 144
Willsher, E. 20, 44, 45
Wilson, Harold 118
Wilson, J. V. 166, 167
Wisden, J. 19, 20
Woodfull, W. M. 76 *et seq*, P
Woolmer, R. A. 124, 137, 144, 145
Worrell, F. M. 124
Wyatt, R. E. S. 75
Wynter, R. R. 126

Yardley, N. W. D. 164

Zaheer Abbas 137, 141, 143, 147